# The Official NASCAR® Handbook

# The Official NASCAR® Handbook

## Everything You Want to Know About the NASCAR Winston Cup Series

HarperHorizon
*An Imprint of* HarperCollins*Publishers*

With special thanks to key individuals at NASCAR for their contributions in the creation of *The Official NASCAR Handbook*: Paul Brooks, Director of Special Projects and Publishing; Kelly Crouch, Editorial Manager; and Kevin Triplett, Director of Operations. At Street & Smith's Sports Group: Steve Waid.

Photographs by PHIL CAVALI and CHAD FLETCHER, Wayne Ebinger, Darryl Graham, Gil Haywood, Don Kelly, Larry McTighe, Gary Shook, Jim Smith, Tim Twiss, and Don Winchester; copyright Street & Smith's Sports Group. Additional photographs in chapter 8, courtesy of Daytona Racing Archives, and photograph on page 86, courtesy of Daytona USA.



*The Official NASCAR Handbook* was published by HarperHorizon, an imprint of HarperCollins*Publishers* Inc. Horizon is a registered trademark used under license from Forbes Inc.

FIRST EDITION

Designed by Christina Bliss

ISBN 0-06-107318-0

98 99 00 01 02 10 9 8 7 6 5 4 3 2 1

# CONTENTS

# INTRODUCTION

## Welcome to What You Might Call "NASCAR 101"

This handbook, *The Official NASCAR Handbook: Everything You Want to Know About the NASCAR Winston Cup Series*, has been created to give you a thorough overview of the NASCAR Winston Cup Series, its races, its cars, its competitors, and just about everything else. This is your ultimate guide to the exciting world of NASCAR Winston Cup racing.

It's simple and easy to use. There's nothing daunting about it; rather, it's fun! Inside you'll find easy-to-read descriptions of what the NASCAR Winston Cup Series is all about, from what the flags mean to the details of a stock car.

If you are just starting to get interested in NASCAR Winston Cup racing, you will find this handbook invaluable, as it will help you better understand and enjoy the sport. If you are a tried-and-true "gearhead" who can tell your friends what a compression ratio is, well…same thing.

This handbook takes you through the entire spectrum of NASCAR Winston Cup racing. And we break it all down for you for easy reading and understanding.

In part one, you'll learn how the actual competition in NASCAR Winston Cup racing works. You'll learn how many cars start a race, what pit strategies are used by teams, pit stop procedures, the meanings of the colorful flags, and why and when they're used (you'd be surprised).

In part two, you'll find out what it takes to be a NASCAR Winston Cup driver and discover what being a crew chief is all about. You'll see just who exactly makes up a racing crew—and what they do. Also, you'll learn about the responsibilities NASCAR officials have during the course of an event weekend.

Part three presents a fairly brief history of NASCAR and the NASCAR Winston Cup Series, telling you about the NASCAR Winston Cup championship, including how the point system works and what awards are available to the drivers.

What's offered in part four is an overview of how teams prepare for a race, go through NASCAR inspection, practice, qualify, and we'll even take you inside a drivers' meeting.

Ever wonder just what a "stock" car is all about? In part five, you'll discover that a NASCAR Winston Cup car may look something like the family car, but it's actually not very close to it. The body, chassis, and required parts, the engine and all its inner workings, the "setup" of a stock car—shock absorbers, springs, weight distribution, and more—and all the safety features will be revealed. And you can get the lowdown on a "show" car, too.

Want to know the differences in the speedways that make up the NASCAR Winston Cup circuit? You'll find out in part six. If you are a veteran fan, you know what to take to a track (drinks, food, sunscreen, etc.) for a race and how to behave. If you don't, well, we'll tell you.

There's more to the finish of a race than just the checkered flag (see chapter two). Want to know what really happens in victory lane after a NASCAR Winston Cup race? Do you know when a race is actually considered "official"? And just where does everyone in the pits and garage area go when the race is over, and how do they get there? Part seven will clue you in.

*The Official NASCAR Handbook: Everything You Want to Know About the NASCAR Winston Cup Series* will tell you how to get more information and enjoyment out of NASCAR Winston Cup racing by directing you to the top media outlets, such as television networks, weekly television shows, the top magazines and newspapers, and even cyberspace on NASCAR Online. Also, there's a handy list of track addresses and phone numbers and a glossary of racing terms (do you know what "marbles" are?) that you should know.

If all that isn't enough, you may also find a few surprises inside.

This handbook was produced under the direction of NASCAR, which means what's inside is the straight scoop. Responsible for most of the content were staff members of Street & Smith's Sports Group's *NASCAR Winston Cup Scene*, the nation's largest and most respected motorsports newspaper. Steve Waid, Tom Jensen, Art Weinstein, and Gary McCredie, all veteran racing writers, put the words together. Can't get much better than those guys.

So go ahead, get started...fire up your engine and go racing through the pages of *The Official NASCAR Handbook: Everything You Want to Know About the NASCAR Winston Cup Series*! You'll get a first-class education in NASCAR Winston Cup racing and have a whole lot of fun getting there!

NASCAR

PART ONE

# 1 COMPETITION

THE GREEN FLAG

WHAT DO THE FLAGS MEAN?

THE PITS

STRATEGY

CHAPTER ONE

# 1 THE GREEN FLAG

This is what we're here for. The pace car has ducked onto pit road leaving just a few hundred yards between the field and the start/finish line. The practice. The qualifying. The anticipation.

Every sport has it. The jump ball. The kickoff. The face-off. NASCAR has it too.

Forty-plus cars lined up double file traveling at one-third the speed they will be carrying the next time they come by this same spot. Thousands of fans on their feet and millions more at home on the edge of their seats.

Engines rev. And then it flies. RPMs rise: 3,000, 4,000, 5,000. Cars shoot to the right. They roar under the flag stand.

The acceleration breeds exhilaration. They have all just received the green flag.

## -------Making It

The number of teams that enter a race is limitless. However, the number of teams that *make* the race is limited.

In a typical NASCAR Winston Cup Series race, the maximum number of cars eligible to make the field is forty-three. The fastest thirty-six cars make the field on speed. The next four "provisional" positions will go in order to any car owners with drivers in the top twenty-five in the car owner point standings. Provisionals used while in the top twenty-five do not count against a team's season maximum of eight. If no drivers in the top twenty-five remain, the next two spots go to the car owners outside the top twenty-five in points already not in the field.

A forty-third spot goes to the car owner whose driver is the most recent NASCAR Winston Cup champion not otherwise in the field. If all champions already are in the field, the forty-third spot goes to the next car owner outside the top twenty-five (but not out of the top forty) who didn't otherwise make the field.

## --------Lining Up

The starting lineup—also known as the starting grid—for a race is locked in after qualifying. The cars line up behind the pace car on pit road before the start of the race. All forty-two (or forty-three) positions line up, double file, with the odd-numbered qualifiers (one, three, five, seven, etc.) on the inside row and even-numbered qualifiers (two, four, six, eight, etc.) on the outside.

PIT STOP

***The pole winner is allowed to choose either the inside or outside starting spot on the front row. However, the pole winner traditionally chooses the inside spot.***

There are often last-minute changes, usually brought about by accidents and/or driver changes. NASCAR rules dictate that if a driver crashes his primary car in practice after he's already qualified and the team has to turn to a backup vehicle, then the new car must start from the rear of the field. Also, if a driver change is made just before the start of an event, that car must move to the end of the line. In either of these instances the cars will roll off the starting grid in their original, earned position. Only when every car has pulled onto the track will these cars drop back to the rear of the field.

PIT STOP

***In the rare instance in which rain washes out both days of qualifying, the starting lineup is set according to a formula. The top spots***

*go to the top thirty-five teams in the current car owner point standings (in order, of course), then the reigning NASCAR Winston Cup Series champion, and then the drivers who have won a race in the current and/or preceding year if they are not already in the field via the two aforementioned procedures. The final spots are based on the race entry forms sent in by race teams and their postmarks (which offers quite an incentive for teams to return them as soon as possible). In the event of same-day postmarks, the team ranked higher in the points gets the preferred starting spot.*

*A full pack of cars takes the green flag at the start of the race.*

## --------Get Ready

On race day, after the drivers are introduced to the crowd, they head to their cars to strap in for a day's drive (unless they are asked to make a parade lap around the track to wave to the thousands of fans in attendance). The teams shut down their generators, which are hooked up to the cars to keep the oil warm for optimal performance of their seven-hundred-plus horsepower engines. The drivers actually have a moment to collect their thoughts while the prerace ceremonies are concluding.

## --------Get Set

Then the gentlemen start their engines. They sit idle for a couple of minutes to bring all the car's fluids and lubricants to

*The field is lined up and ready to pull off pit road for the start of a race.*

the proper temperature. The drivers occupying the front row signal the NASCAR official standing on pit road at the head of the field when they are ready.

**The NASCAR official on pit road radios to the control tower: "Tower, we're ready."**

**Race control replies: "Okay, pace car, let's roll them off. Third time by."**

The front pace car rolls out with the first eleven rows in tow. The second pace car moves out in front of row twelve with the rest of the field behind. The reason for two pace cars is simple—safety. NASCAR institutes a pit road speed (see chapter 3) at every race track. The pace cars pace the field at pit road speed to help the drivers find the correct tachometer reading. Two pace cars ensure that the entire field (i.e., the cars in the back half of the field) receives the same opportunity to get a proper reading. When the pace car reaches pit road speed, the driver illuminates the flashing yellow lights on top of the pace car to let all drivers in the field know that they are now running at maximum pit road speed. The lights are always extinguished with one lap to go before the green is waved.

After the second pace lap, the second pace car drops off the track onto pit road and the field draws together. As the head pace car crosses the start/finish line under the flag stand, the flashing lights on its roof are turned off, signaling the field that the next time they come back around, they'll receive the green.

Turn one, turn two, turn three, the caution car pulls off. The track is ready. The field is ready. The fans are ready.

## --------Go

And the green flag flies.

## --------Restarts

The drivers see the green flag again only if there is a caution period, of which there is usually at least one or two over the course of a four-hundred- or five-hundred-mile race. If there happens to be a caution period, drivers are alerted by a yellow flag from the starter (see chapter 2) and yellow lights around the race track. When the caution period is over and the race is started again, there are certain rules to which drivers must adhere.

First, all restarts are single file until lapping has begun on the race track, which occurs when any car in the field is passed by the race leader. Once that happens, restarts are double file with lead lap cars at the front of the outside line and lapped cars (one lap or more down) on the inside line or behind the lead lap cars. Don't always assume that the first car(s) on the outside is automatically the leader of the race. Oftentimes that car (or cars) is nearly a full lap down but is still on the lead lap in front of the leader.

There are two special rules, the 25-Lap Rule and the 10-Lap Rule, regarding restarts in the late stages of a NASCAR Winston Cup Series race that have been implemented to enhance the competition among the leaders.

### THE 25-LAP RULE

On restarts with fewer than twenty-five laps left in any NASCAR Winston Cup race, *only* lead lap cars line up in the outside row. All other cars (down one or more laps) line up on the inside.

### THE 10-LAP RULE

All restarts with fewer than ten laps left in any NASCAR Winston Cup race will be single file with lead lap cars in front.

CHAPTER TWO

# 2 WHAT DO THE FLAGS MEAN?

Since the beginning of time, flags have represented countries, groups, clubs, armies, and just about anything else that brought together more than one person, place, or thing for a cause.

Flags are also used to communicate when there may not be a place or a time for verbal conversation.

A matador doesn't wave a green cape in front of a bull (wouldn't have quite the same flair, would it?). A soldier wanting to discuss things with the enemy doesn't walk across a minefield holding a black flag. Pirates roaming the open seas in the early eighteenth century didn't fly flags with cute little daisies on them.

NASCAR flags mean something, too. And they all communicate something very different.

## What Do They Look Like?

There are eight flags that NASCAR drivers have to familiarize themselves with. And the waving of any of them means something very important.

### GREEN FLAG

We've discussed the green flag (see chapter 1). Just like a traffic light, green means go, hit it, step on it, pedal to the metal. The green flag starts and restarts the race.

Once the starting (green) flag is waved the car in the second position cannot reach the start/finish line before the pole sitter (see chapter 11) or a penalty will be assessed by NASCAR.

After the race starts, the green flag is not displayed again until there is a caution period. In that instance, the green flag is thrown to restart the race.

PIT STOP

*For most NASCAR Winston Cup races, the official starter (the person who waves the flags) seldom actually starts the race. That privilege usually goes to a specially designated person*

*The starter of a race often is not a NASCAR official.*

*(like an executive from the event sponsor, a politician, a celebrity, or even a fan who happens to win a contest).*

### BLUE FLAG WITH DIAGONAL ORANGE STRIPE

Okay, you're a NASCAR driver and you're barreling down the front stretch at over 150 miles per hour. But you're not running as well as you would like. In fact, you're a couple of laps down. You look up and the starter is showing you a blue flag with an orange diagonal stripe. What do you do?

Drivers have to be aware of the meaning of all the flags. But this flag is the one most new NASCAR fans see the most and probably know the least about.

It is the "passing flag" or "move-over flag" and is thrown by the starter to the cars running one lap or more down, telling them to show courtesy to the lead lap cars racing around them. These cars must prepare to yield to approaching traffic.

### YELLOW FLAG

Like a yellow traffic light, the yellow flag means take caution and proceed carefully.

The yellow flag is displayed to warn drivers to slow down and use caution when proceeding on the race track. The first car passing the starter immediately following the occurrence of the caution will receive the yellow flag. All cars receiving the yellow flag at the start/finish line will slow down. Until each car crosses the start/fin-

*The caution flag is thrown to a pack of cars coming across the start/finish line.*

ish line, drivers can continue to improve their position. Once they cross the line they will hold their position and form a single line behind the lead car. The pace car will come back out onto the race track in front of the pack until the green flag is ready to fly again.

Yellow flags are used to slow the pace of the race. The determination of what constitutes a reason for a caution period lies in the hands of the NASCAR officials in the race control tower.

PIT STOP *To signify the halfway point of each race the starter crosses any two flags and displays them to the field.*

## RED FLAG

Okay, we've had green and we've had yellow, so what about red? A red light at an intersection means a driver needs to stop. Same with the red flag.

A red flag signifies the event must come to an immediate halt, regardless of the position of the cars on the race track. Regardless of the reason (i.e., inclement weather or an accident), a red flag is displayed to a field when it is determined by NASCAR officials that track conditions are not conducive to allowing the event to continue. Cars are brought to a halt in a designated area or right on the race track and repairs or service of any type is prohibited. Also, all work must stop immediately on cars in the pits and/or garage area and cannot resume until the red flag period comes to an end and the race is restarted.

## BLACK FLAG

You're driving in a race and coming through the tri-oval of a superspeedway. You look up at the starter's stand and see your car number on the flashing electronic

*When a red flag is thrown, the cars must come to a complete stop.*

board (which is mounted on the starter's stand) and the starter is waving a black flag and pointing at you. What does this mean?

Well, for any number of reasons, it means you are to report to your pit immediately. Your car could be smoking, you could be going too slow on the race track, you could have passed on the wrong side on the restart, and so on. Whichever, you need to report to the pits immediately to correct the situation.

*The checkered flag is waved to signify the end of the race.*

The black flag is the last flag a driver wants to see because it indicates that there is probably something wrong with the car. There is no flag they want to see less than the black flag, except the...

### BLACK FLAG WITH WHITE CROSS

This flag simply means one thing. The driver has not responded to the black flag and is being notified by NASCAR officials that his laps will no longer be counted until he heads to the pits.

### WHITE FLAG

No matter how long or how short a race is, the white flag appears one time and one time only—when there is one lap left in the event. The white flag indicates that the leader has started his or her last lap, which is, therefore, the final lap of the race.

Once the white flag is displayed, cars may not receive any assistance except in the form of a regular pit stop.

PIT STOP

*For example, if a car runs out of gas on the last lap of a race and cannot make it to the finish line, it would have to come into the pits to receive fuel. The driver's team would not be permitted to physically push him across the start/finish line.*

### CHECKERED FLAG

When the checkered flag waves, the race has been completed.

# CHAPTER THREE 3 THE PITS

## ------Life in the Pits

Many say that races are won and lost in the pits. The simple fact that the outcome of something that may last more than three hours can hinge on something that can happen in twenty seconds is one of the amazing aspects of NASCAR racing.

It could be called anything from "organized chaos" to a "mechanical ballet." But one adjective for it on which everyone would agree is "crucial." Nowhere else in a race can a driver and team make up as

A pit crew leaps to the car as it pulls into the pit stall.

much ground in as short amount of time as on a pit stop. It is there they can go from 1st to 14th or 20th to 3rd in the time it takes most people to tie their shoes.

Here we will examine this "race within the race."

## --------Procedure

This part is simple. At least the procedure of when a team will make a pit stop is simple: anytime they really need to. See, there is no limit to the number of pit stops a team can make in a NASCAR Winston Cup race, only a limit on what they can do and how they can do it.

### *WHEN?*

This would seem to be an easy decision and sometimes is. Teams try to pit during a caution period because most can come in without losing a lap. They've got time to service, get out, and catch up with the rest of the field before the pace car comes back around. And, after all, it's not hard for a team to decide to bring its driver in for a pit stop if calculations show he is about to run out of gas soon or if the tires are almost worn out.

Pitting under a green flag is when the decision to pit turns into strategy. If a driver pits under green he risks getting lapped. This could prove costly if a caution flag comes out right after he has pitted. With the other cars pitting during the caution period he would lose the opportunity to make up the lost positions.

Some questions a crew chief might ask himself are, "When is the leader going to pit?" or, if his driver is the leader, "How close are the second- and third-place cars to pitting?" "Will he take four tires or two?" "Gas and go?"

It doesn't matter; these decisions have to be made in a timely manner, and once they are made, teams have a certain routine they follow.

### *HOW?*

Once a crew chief decides to bring his driver down pit road for service (a decision relayed by two-way radio), the driver will move to the inside line. If he's not already there, he'll use hand signals to let the driv-

*The team members work together to get the car out of the pits as fast as possible.*

ers behind him know that he will be slowing down and pulling into the pits.

The driver has to slow down because, in the interest of safety, there is a speed limit on pit road. The speed limit varies from track to track depending on the size of the facility, but is usually between 35 and 55 mph. But get this... NASCAR race cars *do not* have speedometers. Drivers must gauge their speed by monitoring the tachometer for the number of revolutions per minute (RPM) the engine is turning. As we mentioned in chapter 1, the drivers get the correct RPM reading during the pace laps before the start of the race. Drivers who enter the pits and proceed down pit road faster than the speed limit will be held in their pit box for an additional fifteen seconds by NASCAR officials before being released to return to the track. NASCAR officials monitor pit road speed from the control tower.

PIT STOP

***At most race tracks fans can rent or purchase radio scanners to listen in on their favorite teams communicating with their drivers.***

### WHERE?

Each team has a designated pit box that is chosen by the team after they officially qualify for the race. The pits are selected in order of the way each team qualifies for each particular race. The pole sitter chooses first, followed by the second-place qualifier and on down the line.

This pit box is where a standard pit stop must take place and is marked by white lines on pit road. A team is penalized if any standard pit work takes place on a car in another team's pit; that is, receiving fuel, changing tires, and so on. The car must be completely in the pit box before work begins on the car. If work begins while the car is in any position other than this, the car must be moved into the proper location and another penalty is assessed.

*The rubber marks on pit road show how critical time is to each car.*

## WHO?

ABOVE: Seven men are allowed over the wall, but others can service a car. BELOW: During a pit stop teamwork is essential, especially in tight quarters.

The pit crew (see chapter 6) can be as large as any team wants but only seven members get to go over the wall during a routine pit stop.

These seven men line up along the top of the pit wall waiting for their driver to make his way to their pit box. While the speed the driver is running now actually may be less than a third of his pace on the race track, this is one of the toughest parts of his job. After a driver pulls off the race track onto pit road, he must keep an eye out for the location of his pits, which is designated by at least two pit boards that usually display the car number and colors. One hangs above the pit box and another is waved by a crew member in the pit box. While a driver is looking for these markers, he must keep an eye on the tachometer (to not exceed pit road speed) while also watching for other drivers who also may be on pit road for service.

The seven men can leave the wall and move into position only when their driver is one pit box away from theirs.

Two tire changers move around to the right side of the race car, drop to their knees, and loosen the five lug nuts holding the tire in place with air wrenches propelled by compressed nitrogen. (Note: These lug nuts are held in place against the wheel by glue that was applied by team members before the race started. The torque of the air wrench breaks the glue seal, allowing the nut to screw on. In the past, tire changers would carry the lug nuts in their hands, on a special loop on their belt, where many of today's tire changers still keep spares, or even in their mouths.

The air guns replaced the four-spoke lug wrenches of yesteryear.)

While this is taking place, the jack man places a jack under the middle of the right side. In usually one to three pumps he has the car off the ground far enough for the tire changers to begin work. The tire changers pull the used tires off the car and replace them with new tires (see chapter 4) handed to them by two more crew members (the tire carriers) standing on either side of the jack man. Once the jack man sees the new tires on and the lug nuts being tightened, he drops the jack and quickly moves around the front of the car to begin the same process on the other side. One of the jobs of the NASCAR officials on pit road is to monitor this process and make sure the lug nuts are tightened properly; if not, it's a penalty.

The two tire changers soon follow as the tire carriers roll the old right-side tires to a waiting member on the other side of the pit wall. As the front tire carrier runs around the front of the car he will usually swipe the grille clean of rubber buildup. The changers grab two more tires to continue the drill on the left side. Losing control of a tire could bring about another penalty. Only two air wrenches can be used during a given stop in the NASCAR Winston Cup Series. Any more than that and a penalty is applied.

*Pit stops have been referred to as "chaotic ballets." OPPOSITE: Every drop of gas is critical to a team's strategy.*

Remington
RACING
STREN
FISHING LINES
Remington
Arms
CAMO
STREN
GOODYEAR
BUTCH MOCK MOTORSPORTS
sikkens
Remington
STREN
Remington
Fishing Lines

PIT STOP *You'll notice that the tire changers and jack man work on the right side of the car first and then go to the left side. This is so they and their tools will be clear of their car and of other cars on pit road.*

While this entire process is taking place, the gas man and the catch-can man are in position at the left rear of the car. The gas man refuels the car with two eleven-gallon cans of 76 gasoline (see chapter 4) while the catch-can man remains in place at the rear of the car to catch any fuel that may escape through the overflow valve. If the catch-can man is not in place when the gas man is, well, you guessed it, another penalty is applied. The two gas cans can be dumped in about the same amount of time it takes to change four tires.

At the same time, a drink is usually extended into the car through the driver's-side window net by a long pole on the other side of pit wall (remember, only seven crew members are allowed over the wall).

PIT STOP *Oftentimes, in the later stages of a race, NASCAR will allow an eighth crew member to cross the wall to clean the windshield and service the driver (give him a drink, towel, etc.).*

The jack drops, the driver slams the car in gear, and off he goes—at pit road speed of course. If he exceeds pit road speed NASCAR will call the car back into the pits for a "stop and go" penalty (meaning next time by he'll have to come into the pits and come to a complete stop in his pit stall—then he can go). A pit stop occurs in just seventeen to twenty seconds for a good stop or, in other words, a fraction of the time it took to read this.

PIT STOP *The only time NASCAR officials close pit road is during the first lap of a caution period (obviously, extraordinary circumstances may keep pit road closed longer). This allows competitors to get back into position to make their pit stops. While the cars are pitting, the pace car continues to circle the track. A NASCAR official, at the end of pit road, "directs traffic" with a "stop and go" sign, allowing cars to return to the race track only at the appropriate time.*

CHAPTER FOUR

# 4 STRATEGY

Picture forty-three cars that weigh 3,400 pounds (race-ready without the driver) racing side by side at more than 150 miles per hour for three-and-a-half hours and after 350 of 400 miles, the leader is just tenths of a second in front of his closest competitor.

The difference between winning and losing may come in the form of a split-second decision by a crew chief. Two tires or four? Gas and go? Wedge in or out?

So, you have cars with the same wheelbase, same engine size, same this, same that. What's left? Where can a team make up ground? That's the golden question, and

Lite
Miller
Mobil 1
PPG
Miller
EAGLE
CITGO

the challenge that teams spend the entire season trying to solve. One place to look is on pit road.

They say there is one thing a car cannot do without and that is fuel. They also say that about tires. The thing about it is, neither group would disagree with the other. Without fuel and tires, it doesn't matter what else a team may have. A team can still function with a lot of handicaps. Not having either of these staples of racing, however, cannot be part of that handicap.

*OPPOSITE: While the driver is doing his job on the track, his team is constantly preparing for the next pit stop. BELOW: Fill 'er up! All teams must use the 76 fuel provided at the race track.*

## Gasoline

There is only one kind of fuel used in the NASCAR Winston Cup Series—76 gasoline.

That standard is in place for several reasons, not the least of which is that if every team is getting the same fuel from the same source with no additives, then checking fuel in the inspection process (see chapter 12) is much easier.

NASCAR Winston Cup cars hold twenty-two gallons of racing fuel. The number of laps or miles a car can run on one tank of fuel varies depending on several factors. The size of the track, how a car is set up

(see chapter 16), even how long one car rides behind another one (drafting)—all can affect the mileage a team will get out of its racing machine. Just as with a passenger car, the drivers (and how they are driving) can affect how soon they may have to stop to refuel. The faster you go down the highway, the sooner you'll have to stop for gas.

### MEASURING MILEAGE

The first thing every driver sees when he crawls behind the wheel is the dashboard. Forget the fact there is no radio or CD player. There's not even a speedometer or a fuel gauge.

Drivers monitor their fuel mileage by a fuel pressure gauge that fluctuates when the amount of gasoline begins to run low. But by then, it could be too late. Picture a driver leading a race but running out of fuel just past the entrance to pit road on a two-mile race track. That could result in the driver being forced to drift all the way around the track without power and fall from leading the event, even dropping a couple of laps down.

How do teams prevent that from happening?

Well, they monitor the weight of the fuel cans used to fill the cars with gas. They weigh the cans when they're full (each holds a maximum of eleven gallons) and when they're empty. Then again, right after a pit stop, with what fuel remains in the cans. These numbers are used by the crew chief to calculate the fuel mileage his car is getting. Which can then be used to determine the numbers of laps they can run before having to pit again.

## Tires

A team is allowed three sets of Goodyear tires (and three only) before the field is set (except if the tires and car are damaged beyond repair in an accident). Therefore, each team has three sets of tires (four tires per set) on which to run from the moment they arrive at the track until they are finished qualifying. A team will receive a fourth set if it chooses to qualify in the second round. This rule helps teams cut costs and helps provide a level playing field.

PIT STOP

*There are two terms to describe tires used in the NASCAR Winston Cup Series. "Stickers" are new, unused tires that still carry the manufacturer's sticker, and "scuffs" are tires that have been "broken in" by running one or two laps on the track asphalt. Track conditions and weather often dictate which kind of tires a team will use in both qualifying and the race.*

Once the field is set, teams, in order of the current point standings, are allowed to start having their tires mounted. As with gasoline there is only one kind of tire teams are allowed to use—Goodyear (the exclusive tire of the NASCAR Winston Cup Series). Once every team has received its fourth set of tires it can go back for a fifth. Once every team gets its fifth set, it can then go back for a sixth set, and so on. No team can receive an additional set of tires

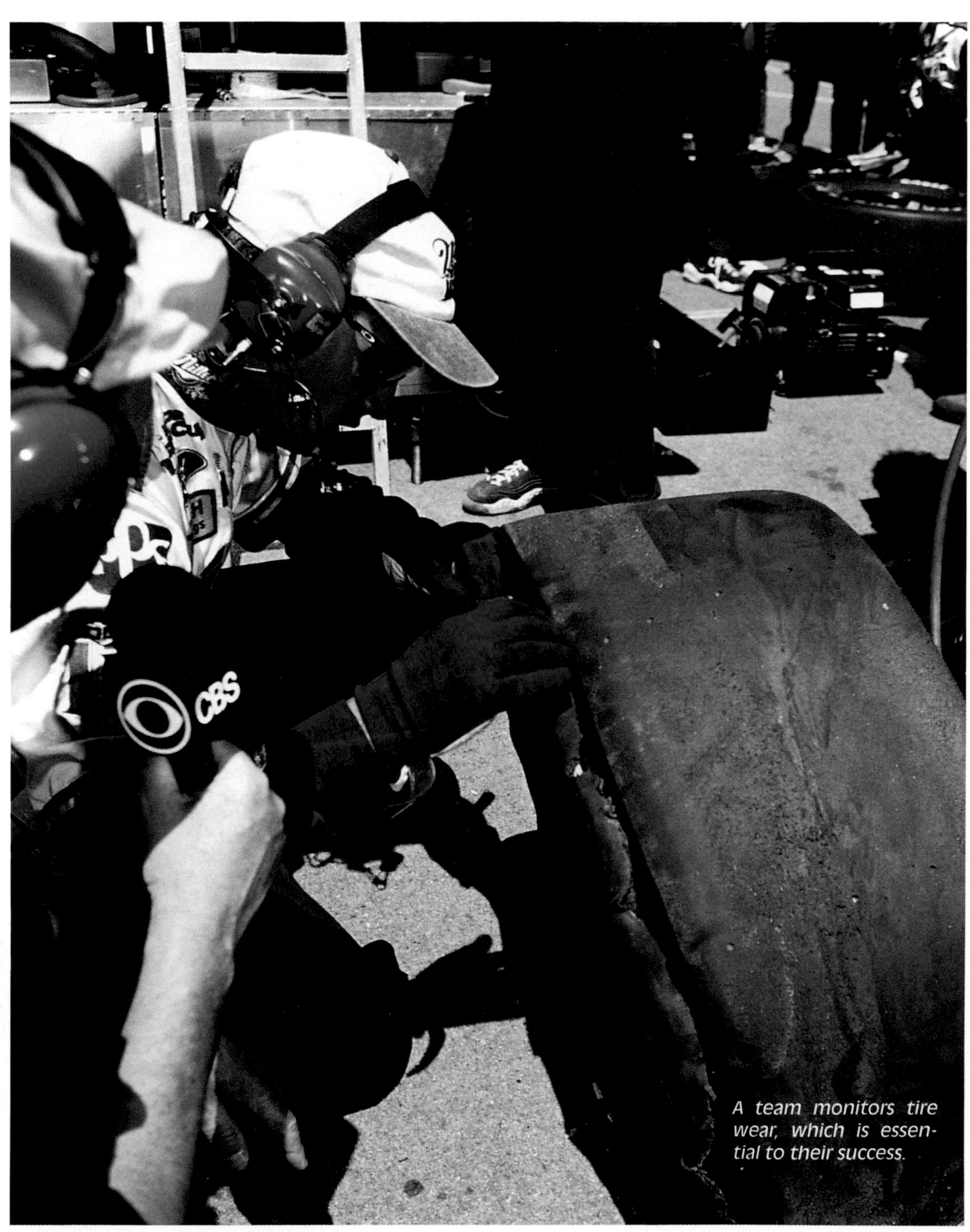


*A team monitors tire wear, which is essential to their success.*

The quicker the jack man gets the car off the ground, the sooner everyone else can get to work.

until every team has at least had the opportunity to purchase the same number of sets.

The reason for this? Cost and equality. Tires are so important, it wouldn't be fair if one team purchased thirteen sets of tires before the next team had a chance to get five. Currently, an average set of Goodyear Racing Eagles costs approximately $1,300.

## WHICH COMES FIRST?

When it comes to strategy, tires and fuel are like the chicken and the egg question. It always comes down to "What will we need to pit for first, tires or fuel?"

If the answer to that was easy, then it wouldn't be such a dilemma. And the fact that the circumstances change practically every race doesn't help matters much either. But caution periods can either create havoc with pit strategy or help build it. It all depends on which card the crew chief decides to play.

## THE DECISION

If a crew decides on a four-tire pit stop, then fuel is not a factor. It takes longer to change four tires on a NASCAR machine than it does to dump twenty-two gallons of gas into the tank, so if four tires are the choice, the driver knows he will be leaving the pits with a car full of fuel. And the majority of pit stops are normal, four-tire changes.

It is in the closing stages of a race, where time, or lack of it, becomes a factor.

Obviously, if a car is running out of fuel in the late stages of the race, the decision is made easier. Or is it? Many crew chiefs will admit this is one of their toughest decisions.

If a crew member has calculated that his driver can go fifty-five laps on a tank of fuel and there are fifty-seven left in the event, most crew chiefs will say, depending on where their car is running in the order, that it's worth the gamble. One of the great things about NASCAR racing is anything out of first place means not winning, and if it comes down to it, most crew chiefs would rather go for the win. What difference does finishing 2nd or 22nd make?

Well, most would *rather* go for it, but most don't. The difference between 2nd and 22nd means 73 points, and that's a huge difference in the point race.

Basically it comes down to, at this point at least, what the leader does. Just as in dominoes, when the leader makes his move, any strategy planned by any other team can be altered. Or thrown right out the window.

The reason behind this is simple. If a driver is running second and there are only ten laps left in the race, he will probably stay out if the leader decides to pit. He doesn't know if he will win if he stays out, but he does know one thing: He won't win if he pits (remember the "if you don't finish first" line of thinking?).

Throw this into the equation: If a car is handling well, his fuel and tires will likely last longer than those of others. Even if you pit at the same time as another car, you may need to pit again sooner, depending on how hard you've had to push your car.

Did you have to come from farther back in the pack?

#### WHAT ELSE?

We have pit stops based on tires, fuel, how many cautions there have been, the last time the team pitted, the last time the teams they are racing for position pitted, how many laps are left in the race, how the car is handling, and, oh, yes, one other thing.

#### THE DRIVER

Like a coach who spends a week drawing up plays and then on game day is forced to throw it all out the window due to unforeseen circumstances on the field, crew

*A team can make up several positions by taking only two tires on a pit stop.*

chiefs often find themselves in the same boat.

A team's pit strategy is often reflected and determined by how and where its driver is running on the track.

And it doesn't matter how many times a driver has come down the stretch fighting for the win, or even if it is his first time. Every situation is different. Different track, different cars.

The only thing guaranteed is, all drivers know they can't win the race just by leading the first lap.

After that, little else is a sure thing.

PART TWO

# THE PEOPLE

DRIVERS

THE CREW

NASCAR OFFICIALS

# CHAPTER FIVE

# 5 DRIVERS

## Just Who Is a NASCAR Winston Cup Driver?

It can be just about anybody. But before you rush out and buy a uniform and helmet and head for the track, there are a few things you should know.

First, it isn't easy. You have to remember that NASCAR Winston Cup drivers are elite stock car competitors who have developed proven abilities. That takes a lot of time and hard work.

*Jeremy Mayfield waves to the crowd during driver introductions, which all drivers must attend.*

Second, for every driver who cracks the NASCAR Winston Cup lineup, there are thousands who don't—and they may be just as able. The problem is, there are between forty and sixty active teams, and half may have the capability of winning any race they enter. So it's something of a numbers game and it means teams are going to hire drivers who have the right combination of skill, dedication, and personality.

## ------The Right Stuff

While it's true a driver can be anyone, there are certain qualifications that must be met, particularly if a driver wants to join the NASCAR Winston Cup ranks.

### THE RIGHT AGE

NASCAR rules require that any prospective NASCAR Winston Cup driver be at least sixteen years of age. Guess what? A valid driver's license is not required. But don't think for a moment a sixteen-year-old without a driver's license is going to climb into a NASCAR Winston Cup car without a substantial amount of experience.

There isn't any particular age at which the drivers enter NASCAR Winston Cup competition. The fact is, there have been drivers as young as eighteen who found full-time employment on the NASCAR Winston Cup circuit (Kyle Petty) while others didn't get started until they were as old as forty-seven (Dick Trickle).

### THE RIGHT EXPERIENCE

Most of today's NASCAR Winston Cup drivers spent years in other forms of auto racing before they hit the big time. Or, in some cases, they came over from one of NASCAR's eleven other series.

PIT STOP

*Seven-time NASCAR Winston Cup champion Dale Earnhardt raced on dirt and NASCAR Winston Racing Series short tracks for years before he got an opportunity to drive full-time on the NASCAR Winston Cup circuit in 1979. He drew attention to himself because of his excellent short-track record and a few one-shot rides in NASCAR Winston Cup races.*

Jeff Gordon, Ken Schrader, and Rusty Wallace all started driving fast vehicles at about the time they should have been on tricycles. Quarter-midgets, go-karts, sprint cars...you name it. Jeff Burton, Dale Jarrett, and Mark Martin are all drivers who gained experience as young drivers in the NASCAR Busch Series.

Something other than pure driving experience enters here. As much as a driver learns about getting around speedways of various shapes and sizes, he learns just as much about cars. This is important. The more a driver knows about how to set up a car, how to get it feeling right on the track, and what to do to make it run better, the more he increases his worth.

*Dale Earnhardt and Richard Childress are one of the most successful teams in NASCAR history.*

Whatever path is followed, as a rule a NASCAR Winston Cup driver has usually spent years honing his craft and gaining experience. His goal is to do well in other forms of auto racing, or in other NASCAR series, to gain the attention of the NASCAR Winston Cup teams.

PIT STOP

***You might ask if any driver has brought his own team—car, crew, tires, and all—into NASCAR Winston Cup racing. The answer is yes. One example is Darrell Waltrip who raced his own car in nineteen races from 1972 to 1973. But when he got the opportunity to drive for noted NASCAR Winston Cup Series team owner Bud Moore in 1973, he took it. He didn't return to owning his own race cars until 1991, after he had established himself as a successful NASCAR Winston Cup driver and had acquired the necessary finances.***

## THE RIGHT STEPS

Even after a driver has landed a NASCAR Winston Cup "ride"—racing slang for getting a job as a driver—he still has to convince NASCAR that he can do the job. NASCAR examines a driver's experience and determines whether it will allow him full or limited access to the NASCAR Winston Cup Series.

If NASCAR is not satisfied that the driver has the necessary experience and feels more "track time" is needed, it may require the driver to first race on the NASCAR Winston Cup short tracks, like the half-mile Martinsville Speedway (Virginia). If the driver races satisfactorily, NASCAR will allow him to move up to the intermediate tracks—like the one-mile layouts at North Carolina Speedway in Rockingham, North Carolina, and Dover Downs International Speedway (Delaware). Finally, if all goes well, the driver will be permitted to move up to the superspeedways, like the 1.5-mile Charlotte Motor Speedway and the 2.5-mile Daytona International Speedway.

### THE RIGHT LUCK

All the experience in the world won't help a driver gain entrance into the NASCAR Winston Cup Series race schedule unless he has the dedication and persistence to do so—and a little luck on his side.

PIT STOP

*When Kenny Irwin Jr., the driver for the Robert Yates #28 Havoline Ford, heard in 1997 that there was going to be an opening on this team, he saw an opportunity and went for it. He called Robert Yates every day until Yates took notice of his persistence and checked him out. The rest, as they say, is history.*

## So He Got the Job, What Does It Pay?

Unlike other professional sports stars, NASCAR Winston Cup teams and drivers seldom reveal their financial agreements. You hear about multiyear, multimillion-dollar contracts in other sports, but not in NASCAR Winston Cup racing. That's largely because drivers are considered independent contractors and make their own individual deals with their car owners. (Believe it or not, a contract is not always signed. A few teams and drivers reach an agreement and seal it with a handshake.)

In most cases, a driver's compensation is based on three things:

- A salary
- A share of the winnings
- Marketing and licensing opportunities

The amounts of each vary in each case. Obviously, some drivers make more than others for many reasons: their success as competitors, their agreement with the team owner and sponsor, and their ability to enhance their nonracing revenue by capitalizing on their on-track success and their off-track popularity.

### THE SALARY

As mentioned, there is no set minimum, so a driver's annual salary is agreed upon between himself and the team owner. Rumor has it that salaries start in six figures but can range to nearly seven figures.

### A SHARE OF THE WINNINGS

This is based broadly on what money the team wins at each race—and the better it finishes, the more it wins. The driver and the team owner agree on the percentages they both will receive. It's assumed in NASCAR Winston Cup racing that the driver usually takes in between 10 and 50 percent of the winnings. But again, percentages can vary from team to team. It is obvious why the effort to win, or to finish as high as possible, is intense because there's more money at stake.

### MARKETING

Drivers negotiate contracts with sponsors to make personal appearances and perform many other services, including marketing the sponsors' product(s). Again, the dollar amounts of these contracts vary and not all sponsors offer personal services contracts. But recently they have become commonplace in NASCAR Winston Cup racing.

You may see a driver, crew chief, or owner wearing particular items with sponsor logos (e.g., sunglasses, hats, jackets, shirts). In many instances, they have negotiated personal services contracts with that sponsor to promote that particular item or brand.

### LICENSING

What has become the most lucrative part of NASCAR Winston Cup racing is the licensing of drivers' names and likenesses to various souvenir and collectible products, which range from hats and T-shirts to jackets, coolers, stationery—you name it.

Many drivers work in conjunction with NASCAR, which has huge licensing and marketing departments. However, unlike many other major league sports, NASCAR drivers control and coordinate their own licensing programs. The drivers earn a percentage (royalty) of every officially licensed product sold bearing their name or likeness. This percentage varies with the individual deals made.

*RIGHT: Accessibility to NASCAR drivers like Ernie Irvan has helped accelerate the growth of the sport. OPPOSITE: Jeff Gordon picks up his check for the Winston Million in 1997.*

Winston Million
SOUTHERN 500
WINNER
Winston Million
DAYTONA TALLADEGA CHARLOTTE DARLINGTON
PAY TO THE ORDER OF Jeff Gordon 1,000,000.00
One Million & 00/100 DOLLARS
WINSTON MILLION WINS
FOR DAYTONA CHARLOTTE DARLINGTON
FROM RJReynolds Tobacco Company

CHAPTER SIX

# THE CREW

## Who Are the Members of the Crew and What Do They Do?

NASCAR Winston Cup team members come from all walks of life, but they all have one thing in common: a love of cars and racing.

Let's get one thing straight. Being a member of a NASCAR Winston Cup team is hard work. The hours can be long and the travel can be extensive. And yep, a team member does get dirty. After all, he works with cars—and that means grease, oil...you get the idea.

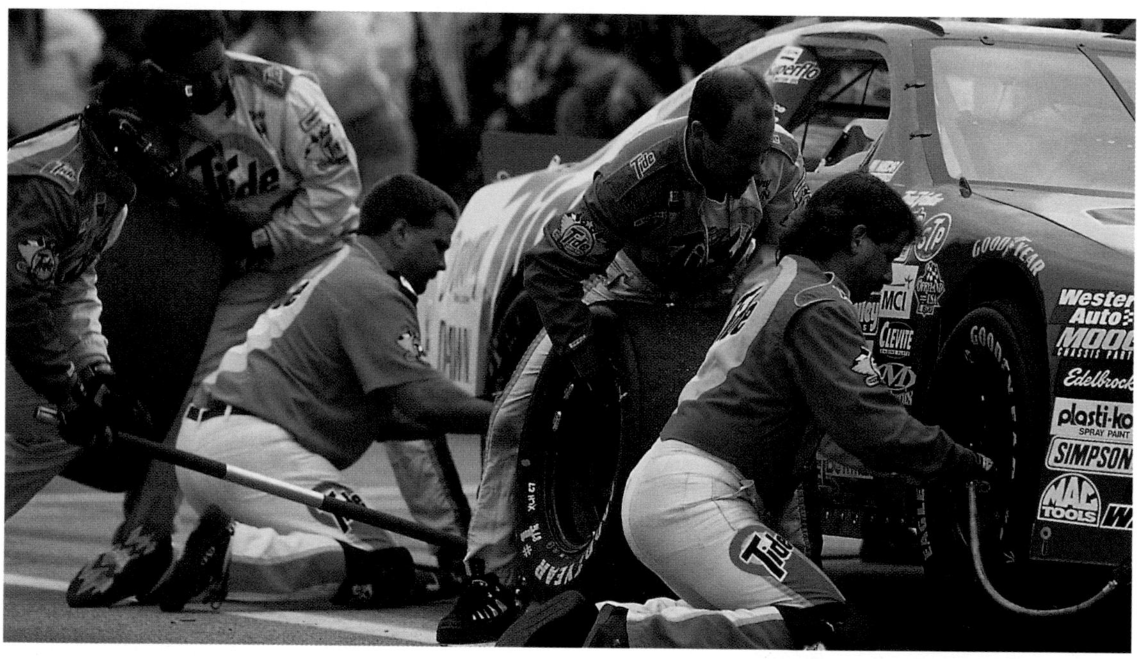


*Tire carriers must have the fresh rubber in position as soon as the old comes off.*

But for the individuals who work on NASCAR Winston Cup teams, there is nothing more rewarding than helping create and/or service a fast car, a car that is capable of winning races. And when that car does win a race, that's when team members smile and admit the hard work and long hours were all worth it.

Today's NASCAR Winston Cup teams are housed in gleaming, clean shops that have all the latest in technology. The equipment used can range from a simple wrench to a very expensive computer or dynamometer (that's a huge, computerized machine designed to test engines).

But nothing works right without the team members' skill and expertise.

## How Many People Are on a NASCAR Winston Cup Team?

It varies. Some teams have many people while others have a rather limited number. The difference is based on the financial resources a team has. Teams with more money tend to hire more people. And the competition in NASCAR Winston Cup racing is so intense it often requires teams to bring certain services in-house when they used to have them done outside of the shop, like engine building and car fabricating. Most of today's teams strive to build all their engines and cars from the ground up in their own shops, and that means acquiring the people necessary to do the jobs.

## What Are the Various Jobs on a Team?

There are many. Some people work only at the shop. Some work only at the track. Some work at both places. Don't get confused. We'll break down the main occupations on each team and explain the responsibilities.

First, we'll start with what is perhaps the most important job on any NASCAR Winston Cup team.

### THE CREW CHIEF

The crew chief is not only responsible for making keen and quick decisions on a race car but is also totally responsible for his team. He is a:

#### Pit Boss

Strategy is a central part of NASCAR Winston Cup competition. For a crew chief, that means determining when to pit and what to do during each pit stop. It also means determining when not to pit. He evaluates the pit crew and decides what exactly will be done on each pit stop and who will do each job.

Imagine a football coach on the sidelines, wearing a headset and intensely watching his team on the field. He's calling plays, he's making substitutions, he's thinking about what to do next. That gives you a pretty good picture of a NASCAR Winston Cup Series crew chief.

#### Coach

He is responsible for the quality of his team, like the coach in any professional sport. To that end, he has to motivate, energize, and communicate. He also has to help develop the talents of his crew and use the right people in the right jobs. Teamwork is key here, and it is the crew chief's responsibility to see that it exists. If members of a team aren't working well *together,* then the entire team will suffer. A good coach in any sport gets his team members to function as one, with the team goals in mind.

*The crew chief is held solely responsible for his team and their actions.*

*Communication is the key to a successful relationship between crew chief and driver.*

But a crew chief doesn't do it all by himself. He usually has a close relationship with his driver. Few NASCAR Winston Cup teams have been successful without the right chemistry between the driver and the crew chief. They have to trust each other. A good crew chief will always try to communicate with and accommodate his driver. After all, it's the driver who has to run all those fast miles in the car. If something is not right on the car, the driver must be able to communicate the problem to the crew chief so he can correct the problem.

### Skilled Mechanic

It goes without saying that a crew chief has to know pretty much everything there is to know about a race car. He has to understand fully how a car works and what it takes to make it run at optimum efficiency.

PIT STOP *Some crew chiefs go well beyond the call of duty and actually perform pit crew duties, such as changing tires, themselves. In fact, being a member of a pit crew and gaining valuable hands-on experience (and, obviously, learning from another crew chief) is how many crew chiefs are born.*

## THE PIT CREW

If you look at the pit area for any NASCAR Winston Cup team, you'll see a lot of people. That's because, as we have said, many individuals who work at the shop are also needed at the track—the engine builder and the chassis specialist are a couple of examples.

But the actual pit crew is composed of individuals who service the car during a pit stop. In chapter 3 we described a pit stop for you; here we'll break down all of the particular jobs in a NASCAR Winston Cup pit crew. As we mentioned earlier, NASCAR allows only seven individuals to go "over the wall" to service a car during a pit stop.

The active pit crew is composed of:

### The Front Tire Changer

Obviously, it's his job to change the right and left front tires.

### The Rear Tire Changer

You can probably figure him out. He's the guy who changes the right and left rear tires.

### Jack Man

He has been known to be the "leader of the pit stop." It's his job to jack the car up so that the tires can be replaced. The faster he works, the faster the tires can be changed. The jack man uses a special rolling jack that is designed to be light (it weighs about twenty pounds) yet powerful, allowing him to raise the car quickly and with minimal effort. When he's done on the right side he goes to the left. The driver takes off when the jack man drops the car.

### Gas Man

The gas man, uh ... puts the gas in the car. He uses a special gas can equipped with a customized valve that fits easily into

*Everything centers on the timing of the jack man. OPPOSITE: The customized valve on the gas can fits easily into the gas port.*

*The wait for refueling after a pit stop is over doesn't stop preparation for the next time around.*

*Tire changers often have to work with many distractions.*

the car's gas port and empties the fuel quickly. When this can is full, it can weigh up to ninety pounds. Most regular pit stops require him to empty two full cans.

### The Gas Catch Man

He is responsible for catching any overflow of fuel. He applies a special container (a "catch can") to the car's gasoline overflow vent to allow him to gather up any gas that flows back from a full tank. The amount of gasoline caught in the catch can is sometimes crucial to a team's race strategy (see chapter 4). The gas catch man may also be responsible for holding the second full gas can on his shoulder.

### The Tire Carriers

There are usually two tire carriers (one each for the front and back of the car). They bring the tire changers the new replacement tires and help guide them correctly onto the

*Spotters: a driver's "eye in the sky."*

lugs. The front tire carrier may also be responsible for cleaning the grille.

PIT STOP

***Depending on the team, there may also be many additional members of the team working in the pit crew. Other important responsibilities are giving the driver a drink (many times by a special pole that is reached into the car from behind the wall), washing the windshield, assisting the tire changers and carriers, filling gas cans, and holding the pit board. But remember, no matter how many people a team has working in the pits, NASCAR mandates that only seven individuals are allowed over the wall at any given time.***

### The Spotter

A spotter acts as a watchdog for a driver during a race. He works from the highest point available at a speedway (i.e., on top of the control tower) and intently watches the race for everything that is going on. He is in constant communication with the driver and tells him things like when and where an incident has occurred and how to avoid it, when he has cleared another car while making a pass, and where the leaders are on the track. Essentially, he sees what the driver cannot see and thus performs an invaluable duty.

### Head Engine Builder

This individual is responsible for building and maintaining engines. It's his job to create the most powerful and durable engines possible. He acquires all the necessary parts and oversees the assembly and testing. Most head engine builders have several assistants because many specific types of

Technologically advanced machinery allows for precision maintenance.

engines have to be built for all of the different types of tracks the NASCAR Winston Cup Series races on. They are required to be ready well ahead of time—and, obviously, there have to be several of them. The assistants may be specialized, working solely with cylinder heads, qualifying engines, or the dynamometer, among other things.

## Fabricator

In a sense, the fabricator builds the car. Specifically, he takes the sheet metal delivered from the car manufacturer and attaches it to the frame of the car. He also shapes and hangs custom sheet metal—sheet metal that he fashions himself. After all the sheet metal is placed, it must conform to NASCAR templates. Most teams have several fabricators.

## Chassis Specialist

While the fabricator works on the outside of the car, the chassis specialist is responsible for much of its internal workings. This individual works with shock absorbers, springs, sway bars, weight ratios

*Many teams build their cars from the ground up. OPPOSITE: Every team's engine is meticulously developed.*

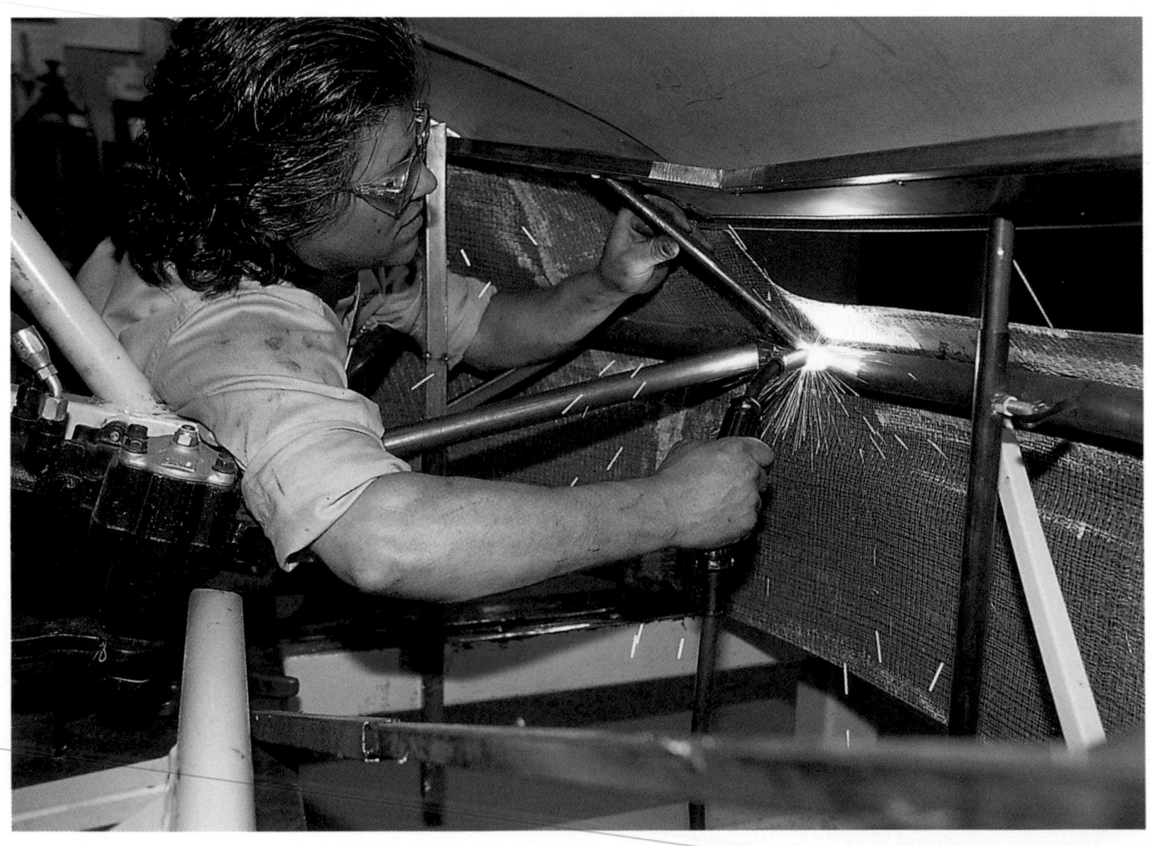

...in general, he's responsible for the overall handling of the car while it's on the race track. Some chassis specialists actually construct the chassis itself.

### Truck Driver

He is the truck (hauler) driver. He's in command of the team's tractor-trailer rig, and that means much more than just driving it. He has to keep it properly serviced, stocked fully with all necessary equipment (from extra parts to food), and cleaned. He transports pretty much everything but the people to and from each race track.

### Gear and Transmission Specialist

This individual builds, maintains, and replaces gears, transmissions, and all the necessary parts.

### Mechanics

Most teams have an army of mechanics, and many of them specialize in particular areas. Some work exclusively on brakes. Some work with tires. Some are welders. Some are body men. Some are in the paint shop. Some are machinists. Some are required to work exclusively in acquiring and warehousing parts. You get the idea.

### Team Manager

The team manager is responsible for the overall operation of the team, which means most, if not all, of the administrative and personnel work. They pay the bills, set the schedules, hire workers...just about everything required for the smooth day-to-day operation of the team.

PIT STOP

*Of course, like any good business, a team has all the necessary "nonracing" personnel, including marketing and public relations representatives, receptionists, secretaries, accountants, office managers, pilots, and even folks who sweep the floor.*

CHAPTER SEVEN

# 7 NASCAR OFFICIALS

How can I get a job with NASCAR?" and "How can I become a NASCAR official?" are very popular and, you would think, simple questions. However, that's not necessarily the case.

## --------How They Got There

The road to becoming a NASCAR Winston Cup official can begin in many different ways.

It often begins the same way that it does for many drivers, in another NASCAR series

*NASCAR Winston Cup officials coordinate the competitive side of every event.*

or other racing circuits. Getting involved in racing at the grassroots level is one of the best ways to learn many aspects of the sport, from competition to inspection to flagging races to even running the public address system. This provides invaluable experience that, hopefully, could take you up the ranks to NASCAR's premier level of racing.

Other NASCAR officials have gained experience through their mechanical backgrounds. It would be impossible to list all of the areas from which every NASCAR Winston Cup official comes, but the first requirement NASCAR looks for, no matter what your background may be, is the willingness to work hard.

## When They Work

Some NASCAR officials are full-time and work in the NASCAR offices during the week as well as attending every NASCAR Winston Cup event on the weekends. Others are part-time, working other jobs during the week and traveling to the events on weekends.

Each official, full- or part-time, travels to each NASCAR Winston Cup event. On race weekends they usually are at the race track for at least four days per week,

*Approximately forty officials help run every NASCAR Winston Cup event.*

sometimes more, depending on the event. They're on the same yearlong schedule as the competitors.

## --------Running a Race

At each NASCAR Winston Cup event, there are at least forty NASCAR officials. You can usually spot them by the red-and-white uniforms/shirts they wear at the race track. Most have a radio and earpiece that connect them all to one central source as well as to each other for immediate communication purposes. Following are the main locations where you would normally find NASCAR Winston Cup officials and some of the duties they perform in these areas:

### INSPECTION

This is one of the most vital jobs performed by a NASCAR Winston Cup official. This is the area in the garage where the weekend starts (all cars are inspected before they are released for practice) and ends (a minimum of three cars are "torn down" after a race).

Chapter 12 will go into much more detail regarding the inspection process, but if you're looking for a NASCAR Winston Cup official, this is a good place to find one.

*RIGHT: Being a NWC official means keeping an eye on everything around you. TOP: The inspection process often includes measurements of the smallest pieces.*

## PIT ROAD

Once the weekend culminates with the running of the race, most everything that has taken place in the garage area for the previous two or three days is moved to pit road. Teams move equipment and NASCAR moves its officials to the area where service will be done on each machine during the race.

There normally is one NASCAR Winston Cup official for every two pits on pit road, monitoring pit stops and enforcing the many rules that govern proper procedure in performing those pit stops (see chapter 3).

Like referees in football and basketball or the umpires in baseball, these officials know what to look for and where to look for it during a pit stop.

These officials don't just wait for pit stops to occur, however. They also relay pertinent information from the control tower to the crew chiefs regarding the cars for which they are responsible. The control tower watches for problems such as a car smoking, going slower than the minimum required speed, lining up on restarts, etc. Pit road officials then communicate these issues to the respective crew chiefs.

## RACE CONTROL

This is the nerve center. If all other areas of NASCAR's domain on race weekends are the body, then race control, usually located

*Communication is essential for officials to run a race.*

*NWCS director Gary Nelson was once considered one of the best crew chiefs on pit road.*

in a tower high above the start/finish line, is the brain.

This is where decisions are made regarding the on-track aspects of the race: When to throw a caution, when to dispatch utility trucks, when to start the race. Practically every decision regarding the race is made from race control.

But, as with nearly everything else at NASCAR, one person is not responsible for making final decisions. It takes a team of several people to make important decisions, often in a matter of seconds.

### FLAG STAND

There are two, that's right, two, starters in the flag stand at each race. Ironically, the "official starter" seldom starts the race. That privilege usually goes to an "honorary starter" named by each NASCAR Winston Cup race track. From there, by messages relayed by two-way radio, the two starters in the flag stand communicate with drivers with eight flags that each have different meanings (see chapter 2).

The starters are also in radio contact with and receive instructions from race control.

### SCORING

Once the race finally begins, how do officials know where each car is running? The answer is through NASCAR Timing and Scoring, presented by MCI.

NASCAR uses four methods of scoring: transponders, electronic button, manual scoring, and scoring tape.

Transponders are small boxes, smaller than the size of a deck of cards, located under the car near the rear bumper, that transmit a signal to the scoring stand every time the car crosses a strategically placed line embedded in the race track.

The second method is an electronic "button" system, activated by a scorer provided by each team every time their car crosses the scoring line. Yep, the scorer pushes a button every single time their car crosses the scoring line.

*Race control often communicates with the drivers through the officials on the flag stand.*

NASCAR officials check and limit the number of tires a team can receive.

The third way is a manual process where scorers tally each lap of each car by hand.

A fourth method, if necessary, is to review a scoring tape that records all information inputted and that runs from the green flag until every car takes the checkered flag.

PIT STOP

*Q: How do NASCAR official scorers determine which driver finishes ahead of the other in the final running order if two fall out of the race on the same lap without making it back around to the scoring line?*

A: They revert back to who was running ahead on the previous lap.

## NASCAR Registration

Sitting in the grandstands during the race and looking down into the garage and onto pit road, fans see hundreds of people: crew members, family, and others.

Who keeps track of all those folks?

NASCAR registration. Every individual who works for a team in any capacity is a NASCAR member and must have a license. They sign in each week at the NASCAR registration trailer, where a group of officials issues credentials for people to access this restricted area.

The job is so large and significant that NASCAR registration relies on a converted eighteen-wheel Featherlite trailer with six computer stations to register the guests and competitors.

All others—sponsor guests, media—sign in through the race track for each event.

## Who Oversees All of This?

The NASCAR vice president of competition and the NASCAR Winston Cup Series director oversee the running of a NASCAR Winston Cup race weekend from start to finish.

Their operation includes a mobile office base in an eighteen-wheel trailer that not only provides an office fully equipped with computers, fax and copy machines, and a weather station but also room to store all the equipment used for inspection and scoring.

PART THREE

# THE FUNDAMENTALS

HISTORY

THE CHAMPIONSHIP

# CHAPTER EIGHT

# 8 HISTORY

## --------How Did It All Get Started?

In the heady days and months following World War II, America began an unprecedented journey toward economic prosperity, with the automobile as a central symbol.

All U.S. automobile factories had been converted to military uses during the war, so from 1942 to 1946, there was virtually no manufacturing of new cars. But there was a tremendous demand for them among the

*Bill France, only the second president in NASCAR history, has helped guide the sport through its recent popularity explosion.*

GIs coming home from Europe and the Pacific after the war.

As domestic automakers began to produce new cars again, it was inevitable that young men would race them. In postwar America, new-production automobiles were faster and more powerful than ever. And drivers wanted to race the cars you could buy at your local dealer, not the costly custom-built racers that competed at Indianapolis and other tracks.

Some parts of the country developed particularly intense passions for racing. Sports and foreign cars were big in the West, while open-wheelers still were popular in the Midwest. In the Southeast, the hot tickets were production-based American cars. And already, tales were spreading about moonshiners—young drivers racing up and down the back roads of the South in souped-up cars, delivering loads of illegally produced liquor.

Of course, some of these young men would butt heads over who had the fastest cars. Sometimes the argument would be settled on the track, sometimes off.

Local promoters saw the potential to cultivate this largely regional enthusiasm into a national sport. Not surprisingly, a lot of people wanted in on the action, which led to the creation of a dizzying number of organizations that professed to represent stock car racing.

Included in the late 1940s alphabet soup of stock car organizations were the National Championship Stock Car Circuit, or NCSCC; the Stock Car Auto Racing Society, which had the uncomfortable acronym SCARS; the National Stock Car Racing Association (NSCRA); the United Stock Car Racing Association (USCRA); the National Auto Racing League (NARL); and literally dozens of others. Just about anybody with access to a track and drivers formed their own local sanctioning body, or so it seemed.

One man set out to change all that.

Bill France Sr., also known as "Big Bill," convened a meeting of thirty-five of automobile racing's most influential people on December 14, 1947, at the Streamline Hotel in Daytona Beach, Florida. The purpose was to form a national sanctioning body to run stock car racing.

*The conference room at the Streamline Hotel was where it all began.*

France had run races under the NSCRA and SCARS banners but wanted a true unified national stock car series. The group spent four days at the hotel crafting rules that would determine how the sport would be operated. The name NASCAR—which stands for National Association for Stock Car Auto Racing—is generally credited to mechanic Red Vogt. The new organization was officially incorporated on February 21, 1948, with France elected as president.

PIT STOP

*Unifying stock car racing was vital to the sport's success, as every circuit and sanctioning body had its own "champion." And getting media coverage in the early days proved nearly impossible because it was difficult for sports reporters and editors to ascertain who the real champions were.*

*Also, purses, rules, and conditions varied wildly from track to track, with races often being run solely on the whims of the track owners and promoters. Sometimes drivers were paid, other times, well...*

## The Early Years

Still suffering from a shortage of new cars, NASCAR's inaugural 1948 season consisted mostly of prewar models racing in a class called "Modified." The fifty-two-race season championship was won by Red Byron.

In 1949, France's plans for a "Strictly Stock" series—the first true precursors of today's NASCAR Winston Cup cars—came to fruition. True to the description, the cars literally were stock cars, with no modifications allowed.

The first Strictly Stock race of the 1949 season was a two-hundred-lapper at the long-defunct Charlotte Speedway. And it brought with it thirty-three cars, about thirteen thousand spectators, a $5,000 purse, the very first rules controversy in NASCAR history, and arguably the first chapter in the NASCAR legend.

Glenn Dunnaway won the Charlotte race in a 1947 Ford set up to haul moonshine. It was determined that the car had illegal rear springs—a common modification among the whiskey haulers of the day—so Dunnaway was disqualified and the win was given to Jim Roper and his 1949 Mercury.

The Strictly Stock series would host a total of eight races in 1949, with Byron again taking the championship, ahead of Lee Petty and Bob Flock.

Competing in the first series was almost every American automobile manufacturer: Buick, Cadillac, Chevrolet, Chrysler, Ford, Hudson, Kaiser, Lincoln, Mercury, Nash, Oldsmobile, Plymouth. And from the very start, the series had a female driver, Sara Christian, who finished 13th in the points.

## Big Changes Already

It didn't take long for change to affect NASCAR. In 1950, the sanctioning body renamed its Strictly Stock series "Grand

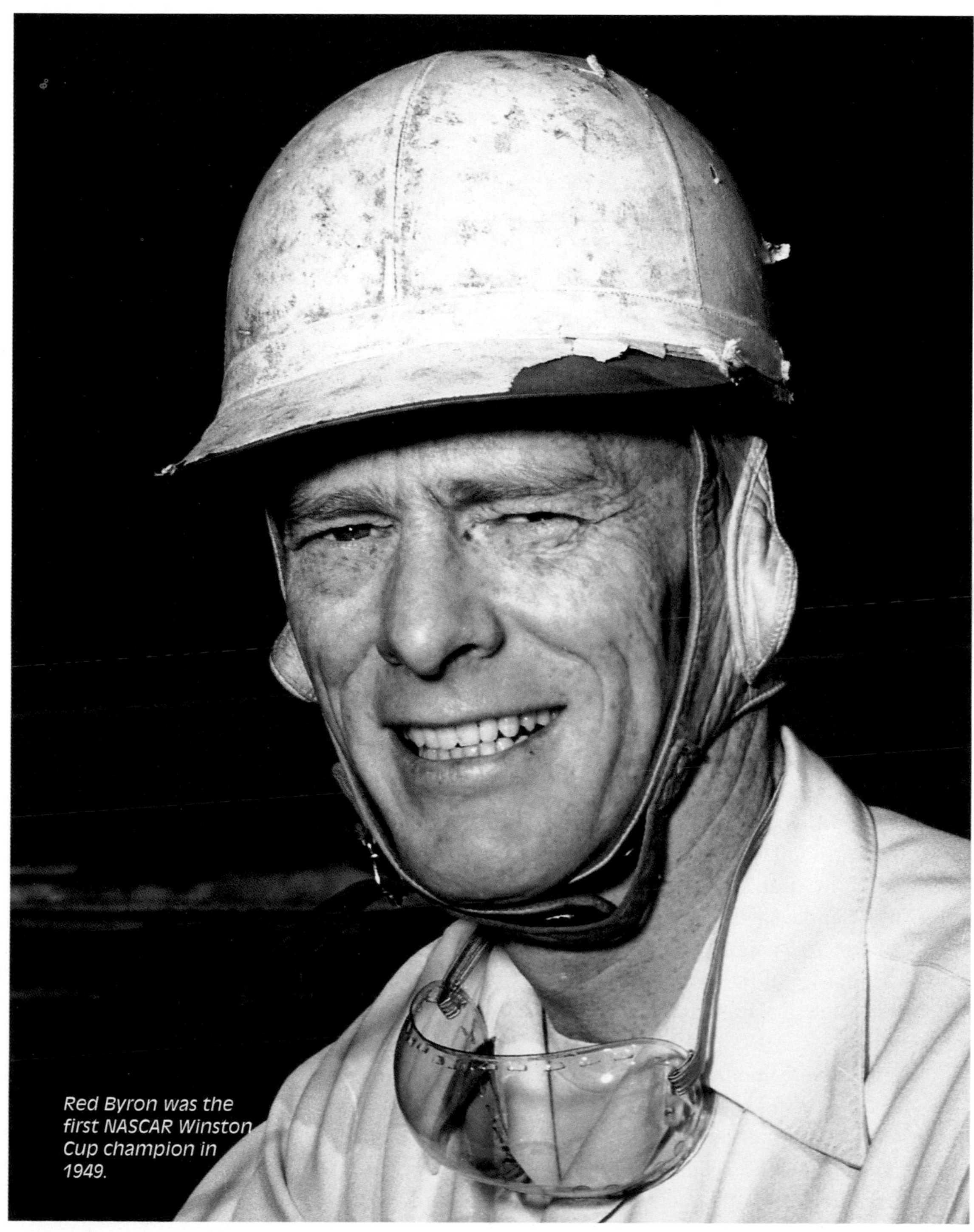

Red Byron was the first NASCAR Winston Cup champion in 1949.

National," a designation it would keep until 1985, and expanded the schedule to seventeen races.

More important, 1950 saw the birth of the first superspeedway. Peanut farmer Harold Brasington built Darlington International Raceway, an exciting 1.25-mile oval that even today goes by the nickname of "The Track Too Tough to Tame."

With France's help, the very first five-hundred-mile stock car race, the inaugural Southern 500, was run September 4, 1950. Darlington has had a Labor Day weekend slot on the NASCAR calendar ever since.

The first Southern 500 had a field of seventy-five cars, some twenty-five thousand fans, and a purse of more than $25,500, a record for a stock car race. Johnny Mantz beat Fireball Roberts by nine laps in a race that took more than six and a half hours to complete.

In its infancy, stock car racing earned a reputation as a bare-knuckled sport—one populated by hard-racing, hard-fighting, hard-living drivers.

Far from the polished professionalism that's the norm today, NASCAR racing had little factory or sponsorship support in its early days. Simple safety advances like fuel cells and full roll cages were years away. This was not a sport with endorsement contracts, high salaries, and corporate sponsorships.

Dirt tracks were common, with the early Daytona races being run on the beach. To compete on the half-mile bullrings that posed as race tracks required toughness and aggression. The great drivers of the day—men like Curtis Turner, Lee Petty, Herb Thomas, Buck Baker, and Tim Flock—ran hard simply because only the strong-willed survived, let alone won races.

PIT STOP

*During NASCAR's early days, it was not unusual to have two, three, or even four races in a single week, if the tracks were close to each other. That's why forty- and even fifty-race seasons were possible back then. Most of the West Coast races in the 1950s were scheduled on the same days that races took place back east, making it impossible for one driver to compete in every race during the season.*

## Getting Established

The simple creation of NASCAR did not elevate the organization to the spot it enjoys today. Far from it.

Well into the 1950s—and occasionally in later years—there were threats to NASCAR's existence. To establish NASCAR's presence, Big Bill ruled with a firm hand.

One common method of handing out discipline was to revoke points or suspend a driver who didn't abide by NASCAR's rules. In 1953, for example, NASCAR revoked points from a number of drivers who ignored repeated NASCAR warnings to file entry forms for races ahead of time.

Such steps, while at times appearing

severe, helped unify the often fractious sport and propel it to new levels of popularity.

*It took nearly three days to decide the winner of the first Daytona 500 in 1959.*

PIT STOP

*Carl Kiekhaefer, a German who made his fortune in outboard boat motors, started the first true high-dollar multicar team. His drivers won twenty-two of forty races in 1955 and twenty-one of the first twenty-five in 1956.*

*His team scored fifty-two wins in ninety NASCAR Grand National races, a record likely never to be surpassed. Kiekhaefer was the first team owner to own transporters to haul his race cars and one of the first to utilize major sponsorship.*

## --------The Next Big Step

NASCAR's next leap forward occurred in 1959, with the first running of the Daytona 500 at Daytona International Speedway.

The thirty-one-degree banking, long straight-aways, and smooth paving ensured that this would be the fastest track on which NASCAR would run.

Of all the many words spoken and written about Daytona—and Daytona alone could fill volumes—none was more eloquent than those of driver Jimmy Thompson. "There have been other tracks that separated the men from the boys," he said. "This is the track that will separate the brave from the weak after the boys are gone."

Fastest qualifier for the inaugural Daytona 500 was Cotton Owens, who ran a breathtaking lap of 143.198 in a 1958 Pontiac that was about as aerodynamic as the side of a barn. This in an era when typical pole speeds at short tracks were in the 65–80 mph range.

More important, the first Daytona 500 earned headlines worldwide because it ended in a photo finish between Lee Petty and Johnny Beauchamp. The race would not be declared official until the following Wednesday, with Petty the winner.

The first Daytona 500 drew more than forty-one thousand spectators and captured the imagination of both the Florida fans and the media. Petty averaged 135.521 mph over five hundred miles, an unthinkable accomplishment for the time, given the skinny bias-ply tires the cars ran on, lack of aerodynamics, and inexperience of the drivers in running at high speeds. Remember, prior to Daytona there was little or no drafting—the cars didn't go fast enough at the short tracks for aerodynamics to have much of an effect.

The fabulous success enjoyed by Daytona paved the way—no pun intended—for new tracks to come on the scene such as Charlotte Motor Speedway and Atlanta International Raceway one year later.

The 1960 season was significant for another precursor to the future of the sport: the introduction of television. CBS televised two qualifying races and two support events at Daytona that year, drawing an estimated seventeen million viewers. It was the beginning of a long relationship that would prove to be extremely beneficial for both parties.

PIT STOP

*Richard Petty claimed his first NASCAR Winston Cup victory on February 28, 1960, when he took the win at Charlotte Fairgrounds, pocketing $800. "King Richard" would go on to be as important to the development of NASCAR as anyone other then immediate members of the France family. Petty, who in his easygoing, self-deprecating manner often dismisses his own achievements as simply a case of being "the right driver for the right time," set numerous records, with seven championships and seven Daytona 500 wins, not to mention a staggering twenty-seven victories in one season and two hundred in his career.*

*More important, his keen understanding that fans are the ones who ultimately pay the bills and make the sport and its participants successful has made him NASCAR's most recognizable ambassador. And he's also set a standard that modern-day drivers are expected to abide by in terms of accessibility and fan appreciation.*

*While the 1950s saw NASCAR's first heroes—guys like the Flock brothers, Curtis Turner, Fireball Roberts, and Lee Petty—Richard Petty was the sport's first true national superstar.*

## Challenges and Opportunities

The 1960s were a time of explosive growth and potentially explosive challenges for NASCAR.

A main issue was safety. Fireball Roberts and defending NASCAR Winston Cup champion Joe Weatherly were lost in accidents during races in 1964, and Jimmy

Pardue lost his life in a tire test. The series of tragedies led teams to intensify their efforts to improve the safety of their cars.

Banjo Matthews, a contemporary racer and close friend of both Roberts and Weatherly, would later retire and become one of the most respected and successful car builders in NASCAR history. Matthews had a well-deserved reputation for building cars that were fast and safe.

Matthews and other car builders helped advance the art and science of roll-cage construction, giving drivers a much safer environment in which to survive a high-speed accident.

Two other important safety advances of the mid-1960s were the introduction of the rubber fuel cell bladder, designed to stop gas tank explosions, and Goodyear's tire inner liners, which made it easier to control a car when a tire went down.

And although it certainly didn't happen all at once, as speeds gradually increased and the cars got additional safety equipment, they began to resemble street cars less and less, to the point where today's NASCAR Winston Cup cars have few parts in common with their street model equivalents.

The mid-1960s were also notable for a horsepower war among the "Big Three" automakers that at various times saw General Motors, Ford, and Chrysler all introduce radical new engines.

Close competition had always been a central tenet of NASCAR's success, and France was determined not to let one manufacturer have a distinct advantage in horsepower.

The same problem would manifest itself in a different way in the late 1960s, with manufacturers building special, limited-edition cars designed to be aerodynamically superior.

The 1960s were also the heyday of "creative rules interpretations." Clever car builders used every trick imaginable to make their cars go faster. This in turn eventually led to much tougher inspections and technical regulations, starting with the introduction of body templates in 1967.

## Shattering the Barriers

On March 24, 1970, Buddy Baker shattered the once unthinkable 200-mile-per-hour barrier, turning in a fast lap of 200.447 mph during a tire test at Talladega Superspeedway. If nothing else, it was another piece of evidence that the sport was moving to another level.

The rapid increase in speed was due in large measure to the development of specialized cars. The Dodge Daytona and Plymouth Superbird in particular sported high rear wings and sloped noses designed to cut through the air easily. Chrysler also manufactured street versions of these cars.

The so-called winged warriors ran only from 1969 through the first race in the 1971 season before rule changes effectively legislated them out of existence.

As cars grew more sophisticated, so did the tracks. Along with the new superspeedways in Talladega and Michigan came a new track in Ontario, California, which was modeled after Indianapolis.

Ironically, the Ontario track became a victim of the late 1970s recession and closed in 1980. Seventeen years later, however, Roger Penske opened a spectacular $110 million track in Fontana, just a few miles from the site of the old Ontario facility.

Other new tracks, including Dover Downs International Speedway and Pocono International Raceway, came on board in the late 1960s and early '70s. As track size and amenities increased, it marked the beginning of the end for many of the short tracks dotting the Southeast, tracks that made up much of the NASCAR Grand National (now the NASCAR Winston Cup Series) schedule.

Tracks like Greenville-Pickens Speedway in South Carolina; South Boston, Virginia; and even the legendary North Wilkesboro Speedway would all eventually lose their NASCAR Winston Cup race dates. Most would live on to host races of other NASCAR series, but the gradual shift to bigger

*Buddy Baker became the first driver to officially eclipse the 200-mph mark in a stock car in 1970.*

*Baker drove the unique Dodge Daytona while posting the record mark.*

facilities was yet another indication of NASCAR's growth.

## --------The Modern Era

Without question, 1972 was one of the most significant years in the sport's occasionally turbulent history. It also marked the start of the so-called modern era.

First and foremost, Big Bill France, whose visionary leadership had guided NASCAR since its first meeting at the Streamline Hotel in 1947, stepped down as the sanctioning body's president on January 11.

In his place, NASCAR's new president would be thirty-eight-year-old William Clifton France, better known simply as "Bill Jr." Under new leadership, NASCAR has not missed a beat, with the younger France growing the sport in much the same manner as his father. Both men were keenly aware of the importance of marketing and promotion if NASCAR was to grow.

The France family transition was far from the only significant change to the sport in 1972. That year also marked the arrival of the first high-dollar corporate sponsorship packages.

Previously, most teams received funding from the automakers directly and, occasionally, modest amounts from local sponsors, such as automobile dealers. But the automakers were in constant wars with NASCAR over rules. If, say, a Ford or Chrysler didn't find the rules to its liking, it would threaten to withdraw its cars from the series, a problem that happened often in the 1960s.

Corporate sponsors were another matter, however. Sure, a beer company or an oil maker coming into NASCAR wanted to sponsor a winner. They didn't care what brand of car their driver ran, though, as long as he won—which in turn eased NASCAR's headaches.

STP and Coca-Cola became NASCAR sponsors in 1972, with STP backing Richard Petty's team and the soft-drink manufacturer backing the Chevrolet of Bobby Allison. Petty would narrowly beat Allison for the title that year, giving both sponsors their money's worth. To this day, STP remains Petty's primary sponsor, and in January 1998, Coca-Cola became "the Official Soft Drink of NASCAR."

Also in 1972, NASCAR revamped its point system and realigned several of its touring series.

*The 1976 Daytona 500 is considered one of the best races in NASCAR history.*

And although no one paid much attention at the time, a cocky kid from Owensboro, Kentucky, made his NASCAR Winston Cup debut at Talladega in 1972, driving his own '71 Mercury to a 27th-place finish worth $1,465 in prize money. The kid was named Darrell Waltrip.

**PIT STOP**

*One of the most significant events of the 1970s was the announcement by R. J. Reynolds, in December 1970, that they would pledge $100,000 for a special point fund for the 1971 season. They also announced the creation of the NASCAR Winston Cup points series. In its first year, the NASCAR Winston Cup money was distributed three times during the season and applied only to races of more than 250 miles. But in 1972, the NASCAR Grand National series was renamed the NASCAR Winston Cup Grand National Series. In 1986, "Grand National" was dropped from the name entirely. RJR pumped millions of dollars into local newspaper and billboard ads to promote NASCAR Winston Cup races, which in turn helped draw increasingly larger crowds, other corporate sponsorship, and better television and radio broadcasting packages.*

*Without question, RJR's promotional and advertising efforts helped take the sport to a new level.*

Richard Petty gets a victory hug from a Winston girl in 1980.

In the mid- to late 1970s, two factors had tremendous impact on the growing popularity of NASCAR racing. One was the Daytona 500, which had two memorable finishes to rival the inaugural race in 1959. The other was, simply, Darrell Waltrip.

In 1976, ABC broadcast a portion of the Daytona 500 live for the third time. The race came down to the two top drivers in the sport, Richard Petty and David Pearson, battling nose-to-tail for the last twenty or so laps. "The King" and "the Silver Fox" staged an epic duel, passing and repassing until the two collided coming off the fourth and final turn on the last of two hundred laps. The two cars crashed together, with Pearson able to barely drag his crippled Mercury across the finish line at 20 mph, while Petty's Dodge sat helplessly in the infield.

It was great drama for millions of television viewers—racing that was hard and clean, an accident both combatants philosophically chalked up as "just racin'."

What happened at Daytona three years later was just as hard, though few would claim it to be clean and none willing to dismiss it as "just racin'." On the last lap of the 1979 Daytona 500, Donnie Allison and Cale Yarborough were going for the victory when they crashed together going into turn three, with both cars ending up parked in the infield, allowing Petty to nip Waltrip by a car length for the win. Bobby Allison stopped at the accident site on the cool-down lap to check on his brother Donnie, and a melee ensued among Yarborough and the Allison brothers, again in full view of a CBS national television audience.

While NASCAR discourages fisticuffs and temper tantrums, the Daytona 500 finish was one of the most talked-about sporting events in America in 1979, again helping boost NASCAR's national visibility.

From 1971 through the end of the 1997 season, Darrell Waltrip was the winningest driver in the "modern era" called the NASCAR Winston Cup Series, chalking up eighty-four victories to Richard Petty's eighty-one. And he has three NASCAR Winston Cup championships, too.

More than just being successful, Waltrip helped define the 1975–85 period as dramatically as Petty did the ten prior years. Waltrip was articulate, opinionated, cocky, media savvy, and exceptionally talented. His success also created a lot of fan animosity. Waltrip routinely beat the champions of his day—Petty, Yarborough, the Allisons, and Buddy Baker—and delighted in rubbing their noses in it, which incensed loyal fans. On the flip side it helped stir up controversy and interest in the sport.

## The Next American Hero

While Waltrip was arguably the first of a new wave of media-savvy, "quoteworthy" drivers to hit the NASCAR Winston Cup Series, Dale Earnhardt was a genuine throwback: a hard case who grew up in rural North Carolina and worshiped his father, a NASCAR Sportsman and Modified terror named Ralph Earnhardt,

*ABOVE: By 1982 Dale Earnhardt had won the Rookie of the Year title and a NASCAR Winston Cup Championship.*

*BELOW: Dale Earnhardt has won more races at Daytona, including the 1998 Daytona 500, than any other driver.*

*Darrell Waltrip won more races in the 1980s than any other driver.*

who died in 1973. Ralph didn't have the resources other drivers did, but there was never a tougher short-track racer.

Dale learned his lessons well. On the track, he was a man who never gave an inch and drove harder than anyone else, a man whose toughness was reflected in nicknames like "the Intimidator" and "the Man in Black." Earnhardt's rough-and-tumble driving style earned him the respect of his competitors and lots of die-hard fans, as well as plenty of antipathy from rivals and rival fans.

He won three NASCAR Winston Cup championships in the 1980s and four more between 1990 and 1994, tying him with Richard Petty for most championships (seven). Six of those championships have come with car owner Richard Childress, making for one of the most accomplished partnerships in the history of the sport.

## --------The '80s, '90s, and Beyond

Between them, Darrell Waltrip and Dale Earnhardt went on to win six NASCAR Winston Cup championships in the 1980s, while NASCAR moved past its growing pains and began to enjoy a period of stability and growth. Of course, not everything was smooth sailing. NASCAR reduced the maximum wheelbase of cars from 115 to 110 inches for the 1981 season, which caused a year of rules controversies and aerodynamic concerns.

Still, after a February filled with howls of complaints from competitors, the 1981 Daytona 500 ended as so many had before: with Richard Petty in victory lane, this time scoring his seventh and final victory in NASCAR's premier event.

By the mid-1980s, television was having an increasing impact on motorsports: ESPN, TBS, and other cable outlets were competing with CBS and the national broadcast networks for rights to televise races.

The increased number of races on television was extremely attractive to sponsors, who obviously received more exposure with each televised race. And the increased corporate involvement in NASCAR Winston Cup racing made televising races more viable, as many sponsors would purchase commercial time during the broadcasts. The net effect was that the NASCAR Winston Cup Series' popularity took off, a boom that still hasn't peaked more than a decade later.

Of course, the NASCAR Winston Cup Series–television marriage was helped along the way by a couple of significant events. The first came in 1984 during the July Fourth Firecracker 400 at Daytona.

It was at Daytona where Richard Petty would win the 200th and final race of his career, an emotional victory made all the more special by the presence of President Ronald Reagan, the first U.S. president to attend a NASCAR Winston Cup Series race in person. Naturally, Reagan's presence and the milestone nature of Petty's triumph was front-page news from coast to coast, and more proof that NASCAR wasn't just a southeastern sport anymore.

The second major national headline grabber happened just a year later. R. J. Reynolds, parent company of series sponsor Winston, launched a new program called "The Winston Million." The idea was simple: RJR would pay a $1 million bonus to any driver who could win three of the four "crown jewels" of NASCAR Winston Cup racing in one season: the Daytona 500, the Winston 500 at Talladega, the World 600 at Charlotte Motor Speedway, and the Southern 500 at Darlington.

PIT STOP

***Prior to 1985, the feat had only been accomplished twice (without the money, of course), by Lee Roy Yarbrough in 1969 and by David Pearson in 1976.***

Bill Elliott won the season-opening Daytona 500 and then headed to Talladega for one of the most amazing races in

NASCAR Winston Cup history. A pit stop for a broken oil fitting dropped Elliott more than two full laps behind the field. Under green flag conditions, routinely running laps in the 204–205 mph range, Elliott made up the two-lap deficit and stunned the field by driving to victory.

The shy Dawsonville, Georgia, native then went to Charlotte, where he was besieged by fan attention and requests for interviews, all of which he found overwhelming. Elliott finished a disappointing 18th at Charlotte.

When it came time for the Labor Day weekend Southern 500, Elliott was surrounded by South Carolina state troopers to keep people away. Somehow, Elliott and the rest of the team managed to survive the intense media and fan scrutiny and narrowly defeated Cale Yarborough to claim the Winston Million—a feat that would not be repeated until 1997, by Jeff Gordon.

*BELOW: Jeff Gordon won the Winston Million in 1997. OPPOSITE: Stock cars today are specially built, high-performance machines.*

## The Future Arrives

As always, NASCAR Winston Cup racing has refused to stand still in the 1990s. The sport's soaring popularity is attributable to many factors: Every NASCAR Winston Cup race is now televised nationally; the racing remains as competitive as it has always been; many fans are disenchanted with stick-and-ball sports; and drivers are more fan savvy than ever.

Plus, there's a great mix of drivers out there. Older veterans like Dale Earnhardt, Darrell Waltrip, and Bill Elliott have established fan bases, as do some of the mid-career drivers like Dale Jarrett, Mark Martin, Kyle Petty, and Rusty Wallace. And the young guys—like Jeff Gordon and Jeff Burton—have quickly made names for themselves.

The success of the NASCAR Winston Cup Series has manifested itself in many ways. Sales of NASCAR licensed products—everything from T-shirts to die-cast cars—are shattering records.

Another indicator is new tracks. Two spectacular new $110 million–plus facilities opened in 1997: Texas Motor Speedway near Dallas and California Speedway about sixty miles east of Los Angeles. Far from the old dirt bullrings, these new tracks are fan-friendly and loaded with amenities.

In 1998, the NASCAR Winston Cup Series raced in Las Vegas for the first time, and new tracks are on the drawing boards for Kansas City, Denver, Atlantic City, and many other locations.

## The More Things Change...

Ironically, at the end of the 1997 season NASCAR came full circle. Fifteen years ago, fans vilified young Darrell Waltrip for his success in defeating their old favorites. Today's most successful young driver and most frequent object of fan taunting is Jeff Gordon, who hears louder and louder boos with each victory.

Ford and General Motors drivers spent the 1997 season debating the rules, which each side says favors the others. This tradition dates back virtually to the beginning of NASCAR, if not the dawn of time itself.

Even some of the last names of today's NASCAR Winston Cup drivers—guys like Petty, Earnhardt, Jarrett, and Marlin—would be recognized by fans who watched their fathers bang fenders on dirt tracks thirty or forty years earlier.

Yes, an awful lot about the NASCAR Winston Cup Series has changed. But the core is still the same, which is why it's the nation's fastest-growing sport.

CHAPTER NINE

# THE CHAMPIONSHIP

## --------The Points System

### DRIVERS

Since its inception, NASCAR has used a variety of point systems, with the current method adopted before the 1975 season. In reality, the existing NASCAR Winston Cup point system is fairly simple.

Basically, a driver earns 175 points for winning a race. Each of the next five drivers receives 5 fewer points. Thus, second is worth 170 points, third is worth 165, fourth earns 160, and fifth 155, while a driver who finished sixth gets 150 points. Positions 7

through 11 are separated by four points, with everyone finishing lower than 11th separated by three points. With a maximum of forty-three starters per race, the 43rd-place finisher would receive 34 points.

*ABOVE: A driver and the car owner each receive points for running in NASCAR Winston Cup races. OPPOSITE: Every driver that leads a lap will earn 5 bonus points.*

Here's how points are awarded, by finishing position:

| | | | | | |
|---|---|---|---|---|---|
| 1. 175 | 9. 138 | 16. 115 | 23. 94 | 30. 73 | 37. 52 |
| 2. 170 | 10. 134 | 17. 112 | 24. 91 | 31. 70 | 38. 49 |
| 3. 165 | 11. 130 | 18. 109 | 25. 88 | 32. 67 | 39. 46 |
| 4. 160 | 12. 127 | 19. 106 | 26. 85 | 33. 64 | 40. 43 |
| 5. 155 | 13. 124 | 20. 103 | 27. 82 | 34. 61 | 41. 40 |
| 6. 150 | 14. 121 | 21. 100 | 28. 79 | 35. 58 | 42. 37 |
| 7. 146 | 15. 118 | 22. 97 | 29. 76 | 36. 55 | 43. 34 |
| 8. 142 | | | | | |

There are two instances where drivers can earn bonus points.

**1. Lap Leader**

Any driver who leads at least one lap gets 5 bonus points. A driver is considered to lead a lap when he crosses the start/finish line in the lead. If a driver takes the lead on the backstretch and is repassed before the start/finish line, it does not count as a lap led. Lap leaders are recorded either at the start/finish line or at a separate "scoring line" that exists at only a few tracks. In theory, the number of drivers who could collect a lap-leader bonus is limited only by the number of drivers competing in the race. In other words, if all forty-three drivers in a given event led at least one lap, then all forty-three drivers would pick up 5 bonus points.

PIT STOP *A race winner automatically earns a minimum of 180 points: 175 for winning the race and 5 more for leading at least one lap, since a driver cannot win a race without leading the final lap!*

**2. Leading the Most Laps**

An additional 5 bonus points are allotted to the driver who leads the most laps in a race. Sometimes, it's the race winner, other times not. Usually only one driver leads the most laps, but in rare instances when two drivers happen to lead the most laps, each would gain 5 bonus points.

Thus, a driver *can* earn a maximum of 185 points in a race—175 for winning the race, 5 more for leading at least one lap, and 5 more for leading the most laps in the race.

For a driver to earn points in a race, he must start the race and complete at least one lap. Occasionally, if a driver is ill or injured, he will be replaced by a relief driver but usually not until he races at least one lap in the race. The relief driver can then run the rest of the race with the starting driver collecting the points.

PIT STOP *At the end of a season, if two drivers tie in points, the winner is determined by who has the most victories. If neither driver has won a race, it's determined by who has the most second-place finishes and so on.*

### OWNERS

Car owners earn points just like drivers because the same driver may not drive for the same owner for a full season. So, that's why two point systems are kept.

The amounts are the same as what their driver earns during a particular race. Therefore, if a driver wins a race and collects 180 points, the owner of that car will collect the same amount. The owners work toward an owners championship, which is awarded each season to the owner with the most points (usually the owner of the car driven by the NASCAR Winston Cup Series champion).

Their points are also used to determine provisional qualifying positions (see chapter 11) and starting positions if qualifying is rained out.

There are two main differences between driver points and car owner points:

1. The car owner gets the full allotment of points earned regardless of who is driving their car (i.e., the main driver or a relief driver).
2. They earn points even if their car(s) doesn't qualify for the race. For example, a 43rd-place car at a NASCAR Winston Cup race earns 34 championship points for its driver and owner. But the car owner of the fastest *non-qualifying* car would pick up 31 car owner points, the next fastest would earn 28 points, and so on, even though the cars didn't make the race.

*Remember: These apply only to car owner points,* not *driver points.*

*Every calculated step can mean more points in the long run.*

## --------The Money

Actually, today's NASCAR Winston Cup drivers have a number of different ways to win money for running in a particular race.

### 1. RACE PURSE

Back in the early days of stock car racing, in the 1940s, dividing up the prize money at a race was a simple affair. The promoter would collect all the money from the gate receipts, the concessions, and so forth. The drivers would run the race.

And when it was all over everyone would discover that the promoter had fled the state with all the money, leaving the drivers without a penny. NASCAR's founding in 1949 guaranteed that shady deals like that were a thing of the past.

Here is a rough breakdown of how the race purse adds up:

### Promoter's Purse

This is money posted by the promoter only. The money is awarded based on the order of finish and typically makes up one-third to one-half of the total posted awards.

### Television Money

NASCAR mandates that each track pay the same percentage of television broadcast rights into the race purse.

*Winning a race can mean a lot of bonus money for a driver.*

## --------Where Does the Other 30 Percent Come From?

### 2. WINNER'S CIRCLE PROGRAM

A somewhat more exclusive payout rewards members of NASCAR's Winner's Circle plan, which offers drivers additional funds separate from the race purse. The ten drivers who won the most races the previous year qualify for the plan, along with the first two winners for car owners not currently on the plan. In the event of ties, the team higher in the point standings gets the nod. A set amount of the prize money is put aside for this plan each race, as well as a similar plan to reward car owners. The Winner's Circle program and other car owner money plans are a couple of reasons a driver finishing 19th may win more than a driver finishing 15th who is not on these plans.

### 3. CONTINGENCY AWARDS

If you've seen a race car, you've seen all the colorful decals applied to the front quarterpanels. Each of these decals has a purpose. They represent contingency award sponsors and their products. In order for a driver

*Contingency decals applied to a car qualify drivers for potential bonus awards.*

or team to be eligible to receive any of the contingency awards offered, the car must carry the decal of the award sponsor and in some cases the product actually has to be used on the race car. Otherwise, they won't be eligible for the award, which pays a driver depending on where he finishes. Teams have the option of selecting which decals they apply to their cars and almost always apply all those of the sponsors who provide them with support.

NASCAR-licensed companies and sponsors put up an almost limitless number of contingency and incentive awards for drivers. The big prize is the R. J. Reynolds–sponsored point fund, which currently totals about $6 million and is shared by the top drivers. This doesn't include NASCAR bonus money. Each NASCAR Winston Cup track donates a percentage to the NASCAR Winston Cup point fund each year. After the champion receives his share, the remaining money in the point fund is divided among the top twenty-five drivers and owners in the standings.

We told you about the Winston Million in chapter 8. In 1998, it was replaced by a new $5 million RJR promotion called the No Bull 5 centered on the same four races, plus the Brickyard 400 at Indianapolis. Drivers qualify for the No Bull 5 by finishing in the top five at any No Bull 5 race and then winning the next No Bull 5 race. For example, if Dale Earnhardt finished anywhere in the top five at the Daytona 500 and then won the Coca-Cola 600, he'd win a $1 million bonus. In theory, RJR could hand out $5 million per season in No Bull 5 bonus money to drivers.

Anheuser-Busch, Inc., has been a longtime sponsor of the Busch Pole Award—$5,000 is awarded at each race to the pole winner and $500 goes to the fastest second-day qualifier. In addition, a $40,000 check is awarded at year-end to the driver who earns the most poles in the course of one season, as well as another $10,000 to his crew chief. In 1998, another Anheuser-Busch brand, Budweiser, took over the pole program, naming it the Bud Pole Award.

In addition to RJR and Anheuser-Busch, a whole host of companies sponsor special NASCAR Winston Cup race awards, including but not limited to these awarded in 1998. It's important to remember this money is *always* paid to the highest finishing eligible driver/team. Try to keep up!

### AE Clevite Engine Builder Award

The top three NASCAR Winston Cup engine builders are ranked based on a point system. The winner of the most points at year-end receives $50,000; second is worth $20,000; third, $10,000.

### Exide All Charged Up Award

This award pays $2,000 at each NASCAR Winston Cup race to the eligible driver who

*Drivers receive contingency bonus money during prerace ceremonies at the following race.*

makes up the most places on the grid from start to finish. Exide also offers a season-ending bonus of $50,000.

### Gatorade Front Runner Award

The leader at the halfway point of each NASCAR Winston Cup race receives $10,000; the point leader at the halfway point of the season pockets an additional $50,000.

### MCI Fast Pace Award

The drivers who turn the fastest lap at each NASCAR Winston Cup race win $5,000. At the end of the year the driver to turn the fastest lap of the season takes home $50,000.

### Plasti-Kote Winning and Quality Finish Awards

The crew chief of the winning car at each NASCAR Winston Cup race receives $2,000. The crew chiefs with the best average finish at year-end divide an additional $38,000 among them.

### Raybestos Top Stopper Award

At each NASCAR Winston Cup race, the eligible driver receives $2,000, the runner-up gets $1,000, and the third-place finisher wins $500. Points are also awarded to the top three finishers of each race (100, 50, and 25, respectively). A year-end bonus of $50,000 is paid to the driver with the most points.

### True Value/NASCAR Man-of-the-Race/Year Award

This award pays $2,000 at each NASCAR Winston Cup race to the driver who shows the most concern for others. Half of the money is paid to that driver's favorite charity. At year-end, an additional $25,000 is paid to a Man of the Year (chosen from that season's Man-of-the-Race winners), and an additional $25,000 is donated to his favorite charity.

### 76 Challenge

If the pole winner at any NASCAR Winston Cup event also wins the race, 76 will pay him a $7,600 bonus. If the driver is unsuccessful, the award money will roll over until someone does win from the pole.

*Bonus money is awarded from several different sponsors.*

PIT STOP

*The biggest 76 Challenge payout to date came in 1990, when Kyle Petty won the GM Goodwrench 500 at Rockingham, North Carolina, and pocketed $284,450.*

### NASCAR Winston Cup Leader Bonus

At each NASCAR Winston Cup race any driver who wins the race and is leading the NASCAR Winston Cup point standings at the end of that race will receive $10,000 from Winston. Just as in the 76 Challenge the money rolls over until someone wins.

If you've ever wondered how a driver who finishes eighth in a race can win more money than a driver who finishes in front of him, here's your answer—contingency awards. The driver with the higher pay probably had more (or better) contingency winnings and/or plan money, as discussed earlier.

PIT STOP

*Prize money throughout NASCAR has skyrocketed in recent years. Case in point: Richard Petty, the all-time winningest driver in NASCAR with two hundred career wins, won $7.75 million in prize money during a thirty-five-year driving career that ended in 1992. Michael Waltrip, who has less than one-third the number of career starts posted by Petty, and has no career wins, already had won more than $6 million (through the 1997 season).*

PART FOUR

# GETTING RACE-READY

BEFORE THE RACE

QUALIFYING

INSPECTION

DRIVERS' MEETING

CHAPTER TEN

# BEFORE THE RACE

## Entering an Event

To participate in an event, first a team must enter the event. This is done by submitting an entry form (provided by NASCAR) to both NASCAR and the promoter of the upcoming race. This has to be done by a certain date, specified on the entry blank. A team can still enter a race after the entry deadline by notifying NASCAR of its intentions with the understanding that the team *will not* receive any points for participating in the event. They can, however, still win money.

## The Early Birds

Each week teams must check in at the race track by a specific time. The time differs from track to track, but it's almost without exception an early-morning hour. With the demanding travel schedule in the NASCAR Winston Cup Series today, the deadline isn't always easy to meet.

On the morning of the first day of each event NASCAR opens the garage (usually around 6:00 A.M.) to allow each team to park its eighteen-wheel transporters (a.k.a. haulers). NASCAR officials mark off parking areas for each team hauler. The defending champion's hauler parks first, with the others, in descending order of current car owner points, following. No problem for the teams in the top five or top ten. If you're, say, number forty-three in points, you have to wait your turn. And wait. And wait.

## Preparing for Battle

Like an army massing its troops and equipment for an attack, the NASCAR Winston Cup area is a blur of activity when the race teams first enter the garage area. About one hour after the haulers park, the

*OPPOSITE: NASCAR Winston Cup teams have to get an early start on the day. RIGHT: On race morning teams go over every inch of the car.*

garage traditionally is opened again for the teams to unload their primary cars into the garage stalls. The stalls are allotted by the same method as the haulers: first stall to the defending champion, and then in descending order based on the current owner point standings. The primary car, which is stored on a hydraulic lift shelf in the hauler, along with the "pit wagon," which carries the team's tools and other equipment in the pit area, are the first to come off the truck. Other essential items that follow include jackstands, shop rags, a water tank, parts, water coolers, and, yes, a barbecue grill. (Hey, crew members have to eat too.)

To say the NASCAR Winston Cup garage area is a beehive of activity after the teams arrive would be a cliché but it would also be accurate. Crew members for the various teams are hustling so hard before a race they'd make a bee colony look like a bunch of lazy, aimless beach bums. Crew members have to push their car through the inspection process. Tools and other equipment have to be set up in the garage area. Various parts on the car need tweaking.

## Practice Doesn't Always Make Perfect, but It Sure Helps

Every sport has its practice time before the big event. Pro golfers head for the driving range or putting green. Baseball players take their turn in the batting cage. Basketball teams have their pregame shootaround.

But the NASCAR Winston Cup Series' prerace practices are arguably the most

*Each piece of equipment is checked for wear before a long race.*

important in sports. You would not, for example, find a top pro golfer replacing his favorite set of clubs with a brand-new set just before a big tournament. A football coach wouldn't throw out his whole game plan. Yet that's exactly what sometimes happens during a race weekend, as teams change their planned race setup for something radically different.

It's not unusual for teams to swap engines if they can't get the car up to speed in practice. Sure, teams have a good idea of what to expect at a certain track based on past experience; crew chiefs keep stacks of notes on such things. But changes on race weekend (unusually cold or hot weather, idiosyncrasies with that particular car, changes in track conditions due to repaving, etc.) can lead a team to make major changes during practice.

Practice sessions also give rookie drivers a chance to learn the track and new driver–crew chief combinations an additional chance to feel each other out.

NASCAR aims to keep practices safe and fair. Teams must use their primary car, unless it's in an accident during an earlier practice session, and all of the cars are inspected before they can go out on the track. If the car is involved in an accident and can't be repaired (the NASCAR Winston Cup Series director makes that call), the team will be allowed to pull its backup car off the trailer.

## Every Practice Session Counts

On most race weekends, teams have several practice sessions available in which to get their cars race-ready, at least one per day except on race day. On the day of first-round qualifying they get an hour or two of practice *before* they have to qualify. There's another session (usually one hour) the next morning before second-round qualifying. Later that afternoon will be the final practice session before the race event, also known as "Happy Hour."

## Why Happy Hour Is Sometimes Not So Happy

For many people, the term "Happy Hour" probably brings to mind visions of people standing around in their favorite neighborhood watering hole, sipping their favorite beverage and chatting with friends—but these days, it probably makes race fans think about NASCAR.

For NASCAR Winston Cup drivers and their crews, the Happy Hour before each race is sometimes anything but happy. The one-hour period is the last chance race teams have to "shake their car down," to get it "dialed-in" so they don't look like "silly fools" come race time.

Seriously, Happy Hour can be quite hectic. It's the last chance for teams to get their car's race setup ready before the big race.

PIT STOP

*"Happy Hour" practice has become increasingly popular, with growing attendance at the race track. It even has its own TV show.*

CHAPTER ELEVEN

# 11 QUALIFYING

## Why They Qualify

There's a very good reason we have qualifying for NASCAR Winston Cup races. There's really no other sensible way to set the cars for the race. If you let the drivers line up on a first-come, first-serve basis, there would be a lot of angry drivers and crumpled cars come race time. If you lined them up in alphabetical order, a driver named "Johnny Ziegler" would never land a NASCAR Winston Cup ride.

Actually, qualifying accomplishes several things:

*Cars line up on pit road to begin a qualifying round.*

- It groups the cars according to speed, with the faster cars near the front.
- It gives every race team, no matter how poorly it has performed as recently as the previous week, the chance to make things right with a good qualifying run.
- It gives the fans an additional opportunity to come to the track and see their heroes in action. Although "Bud Pole Day" was once an afterthought, tens of thousands of fans now turn out at some tracks for qualifying sessions.

## Tick...Tick... Tick...Tick

As with other NASCAR-sanctioned race activities, qualifying goes off with military precision with regard to time. Any driver not ready to compete within five minutes of his scheduled qualifying time may be sent to the rear of the line, or left out of that day's qualifying entirely. Those decisions are at the discretion of NASCAR officials. Obviously, such a penalty ensures this doesn't happen very often. Competitors also face the mandatory prequalifying inspection of their car, and the top qualifiers can expect another inspection following their run.

Every car must pass inspection before being allowed to make a qualifying attempt.

## The Luck of the Draw

The qualifying order before each race is drawn at random. According to one veteran crew chief, a man who deals in precise technical jargon on the job, the positions are drawn out of "a round-ball thingamajig." Imagine the mixer used at your local bingo hall—you know, that round cage that's used to mix up the balls, which are numbered by position. Each ball is drawn in order of current car owner points (see chapter 9). If you don't play bingo—well, the qualifying positions are picked by the luck of the draw. Leave it at that.

Some fans might wonder why it even matters in which order the cars qualify, but there are a number of variables that can make an early—or a late—qualifying run more advantageous. Say you're at Charlotte Motor Speedway and it's a hot, sunny day, but there are clouds on the horizon, moving in fast. The track will start out slick, and the first drivers to qualify will have to exercise caution. But when the clouds reach the track, the racing surface cools, providing greater traction. Drivers with later qualifying draws will post better times. Of course, it can work the opposite too.

But since the temperature generally drops throughout the afternoon, a later qualifying run is usually better. Also, drivers going later in the proceedings have the advantage of watching their fellow drivers navigate the track and therefore have a better idea of what to expect in certain situations.

## One or Two Laps

Drivers get either one or two laps in which to qualify, depending on the track. Why the difference? Generally speaking, drivers get two laps at superspeedways, like Talladega Superspeedway and Daytona

*Qualifying order is determined by the luck of the draw.*

International Speedway, where it takes the cars longer to reach full speed. At other shorter tracks, one lap is sufficient for them to reach their peak performance.

*The fastest first-round qualifier starts on the inside of the front row.*

## Poles Are a Bear to Earn

The first day of qualifying will set the first twenty-five positions for the race. At the start of this day optimism abounds. And why not? Theoretically, any of the four dozen or so cars set to run has a shot at the pole. And, in fact, qualifying often brings major surprises, with a rookie, an old veteran, or an unheralded driver sneaking away with the day's fastest lap.

But in reality, the contenders usually separate themselves from the pretenders in quick order. The cars take off one at a time and run their timed lap(s). While it may seem to the casual observer the cars are all running the same speed, drivers and their crews—as well as knowledgeable fans—can listen to a car's engine and watch the line a driver is running around the track and determine if the car is a contender for the pole. That's quite remarkable considering the difference between the pole position and the slowest car is often less than one second.

**PIT STOP**

*Each pole winner from the previous year gets the added bonus of competing in a special race every February, one week before the Daytona 500, at Daytona International Speedway.*

*The Bud Shootout—formerly known as the Busch Clash—features a special format and, as the first NASCAR event each season, draws a tremendous amount of media attention. It's no surprise that drivers—and their sponsors—desperately want to make this race. As the season winds down, watch for top drivers who don't already have a pole to make an extra effort to grab one, not only for that weekend's race but to earn a spot in the Bud Shootout.*

## Should I Stay or Should I Go?

Following first-round qualifying, drivers in positions twenty-six down must make a tough decision. They can "stand on"—keep—their first-round time and hope it holds up, or they can elect to requalify. The decision is based on a number of variables, but must be made within five minutes of the end of final practice before second-round qualifying.

Weather can be a factor, as noted above. So can the first-round standing; for example, if a driver qualified 26th on the first day, chances are he's going to make the field. If he qualified 38th, he better hit the track the next day for the second round.

There is also another factor to consider. Most tracks are slower in the second round due to oil and built-up rubber on the track. So even if you had a bad time in first-round qualifying, there's no guarantee you'll run faster the second day.

Either way, it's a gamble, because if a driver decides to requalify, his first-round time is removed from the books. If he fails to qualify in the second round, even if his first-round time would have made the field, tough luck; he's going home.

## The Second-Round Blues

No one, but no one, wants to pick up the dreaded "DNQ," which is racing terminology for "Did Not Qualify." Think of the DNQ as NASCAR's equivalent of sitting home alone on prom night—while everyone else is at the big dance, having the time of their lives.

Nothing is more disappointing for a team than having to pack everything back on the hauler and leave the track on the day before the race. So it goes without saying that second-round qualifying, which is full of drivers who failed to make the field in the first round, can be a tense affair. And some simple math underscores the urgency for race teams. For example, if forty-nine teams show up to qualify for a maximum forty-three starting spots, at least six teams will go home.

The best starting position a second-round driver can hope for is 26th, as the top twenty-five spots are locked in by their first-round times. It's not unusual to have one or more second-round qualifiers post better times than many of the cars in the top twenty-five. But, like we said, more often than not the second-round speeds are slower.

By the way, the second-round rules are the same as in the first round. The qualifying order is drawn at random, NASCAR officials inspect all the cars before they hit the track, and so on.

PIT STOP

*The qualifying process for the Daytona 500 is unlike any other race on the NASCAR Winston Cup tour.*

*For every other race weekend of the year, first-round qualifying locks in the top twenty-five spots.*

*Not so for the Daytona 500. There are three rounds of qualifying. Here it goes:*

1. *First-round qualifying locks in only the front row for the Daytona 500.*
2. *Second-round and third-round qualifying determines the starting lineup for the Gatorade 125 qualifying races. The Gatorade 125s are two qualifying races that are run on the Thursday before the Daytona 500.*

*The cars that placed in an odd-numbered position after the three rounds of qualifying make up the starting field for the first Gatorade 125 race. Every car that qualified in an even-numbered position makes up the field for the second Gatorade 125 race. The top fourteen finishers in the first race (other than the pole sitter) are locked in order on the inside row for the Daytona 500. For example, the winner of the first Gatorade 125 race will start third, right behind the pole sitter. The second-place finisher will sit right behind him on the inside row, and so on. The same is the case for the second Gatorade 125. The winner of the second race will start on the outside of the second row with the rest of the top fourteen finishers lining up behind him.*

*This fills positions one through thirty. The next eight positions then are filled by the fastest qualifiers from the three initial rounds of time trials who do not make the field through the Gatorade 125 races. The final positions are provisionals (see below).*

*Got all that?*

## The Last Resort

Sometimes even the best drivers have an off day, or even worse, two off days in a row. Therefore, drivers may use something known as a provisional start to make a race. The main reason for provisional starting positions is to provide a spot for series regulars and contenders who have had tough luck during the weekend and not made the race by speed.

As the number of teams committing to the NASCAR Winston Cup Series for a full season increase, the provisional system has undergone slight modifications to adapt.

There are a maximum of seven provisional starting spots available for each race.

At the beginning of each race season, provisionals are available to the top forty in *car owner points* from the preceding year.

For example, if seven teams fail to qualify for a race (not including a previous champion), the top six in team owner points from the previous season would be granted provisional starting spots. After the fourth race of the season, the *current* team owner standings are used. Teams start the year with a maximum of eight provisional spots available to each of them, although there are guidelines regulating their use. For example, a team could not use a provisional to make each of the first eight races of the season.

Provisionals are available as follows: First, only the top forty in car owner points from the previous year (for the first four races) and the top forty from the current year (starting with the fifth race) are eligible for a provisional. Each team starts the year with four and then picks up an extra every eighth qualifying attempt. They do carry over. For example, if a team qualifies for the first sixteen races of the season on speed, it has six provisionals. If a provisional is used while in the top twenty-five in the previous year's or current point standings, they do not count toward the season maximum of eight. If all of the top forty in car owner points have made the field either by speed or provisional, the next available spots will be granted to the drivers posting the fastest speeds and not otherwise making the field.

PIT STOP

*If two or more past champions fail to make the field on speed, the more recent champion earns the provisional. To date, such an improbable event has happened only once. Darrell Waltrip was bumped by Terry Labonte (the 1996 champion) at the 1997 UAW-GM Quality 500 at Charlotte Motor Speedway.*

CHAPTER TWELVE

# 12 INSPECTION

To make it to the starting grid for a race, cars have to be built, tested, and… inspected. And inspected and inspected again.

Teams can't just show up at a race track, car in tow, and jump onto the race track. As with everything else, a certain process has to be followed. Inspection is probably the most important and crucial part of race weekend each time it occurs. Teams go through inspection throughout the race weekend because they are allowed to work on the cars between inspections.

## Getting on the Track

Before any cars can roll out onto the race track they are required to be inspected by NASCAR officials. At this initial inspection more than twenty officials look over every different aspect of each car entered in the event (see chapter 10): from the engine (its compression ratio and carburetor), to the roll bars (location, etc.), to the height of the rear spoiler, and so on.

Some of the stops on the NASCAR Winston Cup Series inspection line include:

*Before any car reaches the race track it must first pass NASCAR inspection.*

### Templates

As many as fifteen templates are placed on different areas of the car: rear quarterpanels, deck lid, roof line, doors, etc. The templates are used to assure that the body of each car meets the standard design set by NASCAR for that particular event.

### Height Measurement

The height of the car, from ground to roof, is measured. It has a minimum requirement.

### Weight

In the NASCAR Winston Cup Series, each car must weigh a minimum of 3,400 pounds, race-ready, without the driver.

### Front Air Dam

The ground clearance on the front air dam, which also has a minimum height requirement, is measured.

### Spoilers

The height, width, and even thickness of each spoiler (the vertical blade on the rear deck lid of each race car) is checked to NASCAR's requirements (which may vary from track to track).

### Fuel Cells

The size (no more than twenty-two gallons) and shape of each fuel cell is checked.

*NASCAR officials use several tools to check the height and setup of a car.*

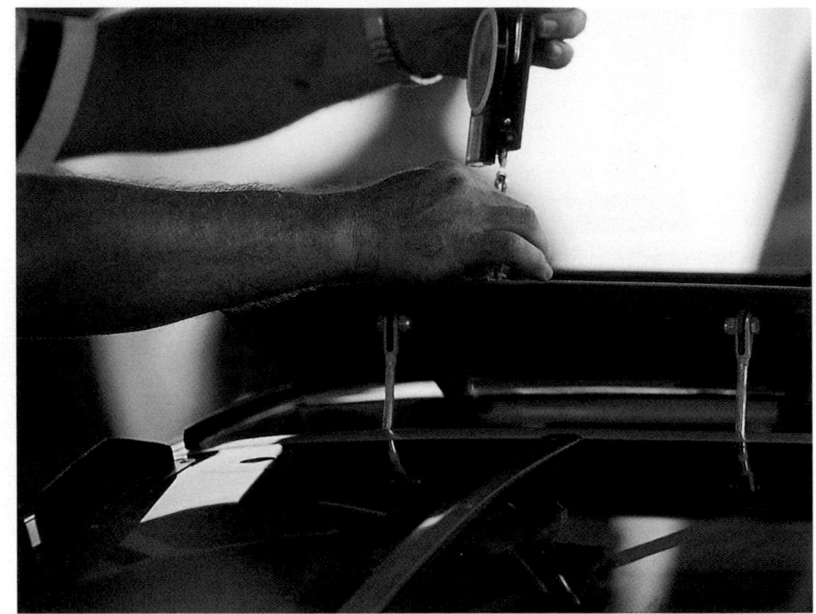

*Roof flaps are mandated on all NASCAR Winston Cup cars.*

### Frames and Roll Bars

Are checked for proper thickness, height, and so on.

### Engines

Are "whistled" to check compression ratio (a mandatory maximum of 12.0 to 1). Cubic-inch displacement is checked as well (following qualifying and the race).

The car then is either approved to be taken onto the track for the first practice session or is sent back to the garage to fix whatever may not be quite right. Usually this is something minor such as adjusting the front air dam an eighth of an inch. No matter how easy the adjustment is, the car is sent to the back of the inspection line.

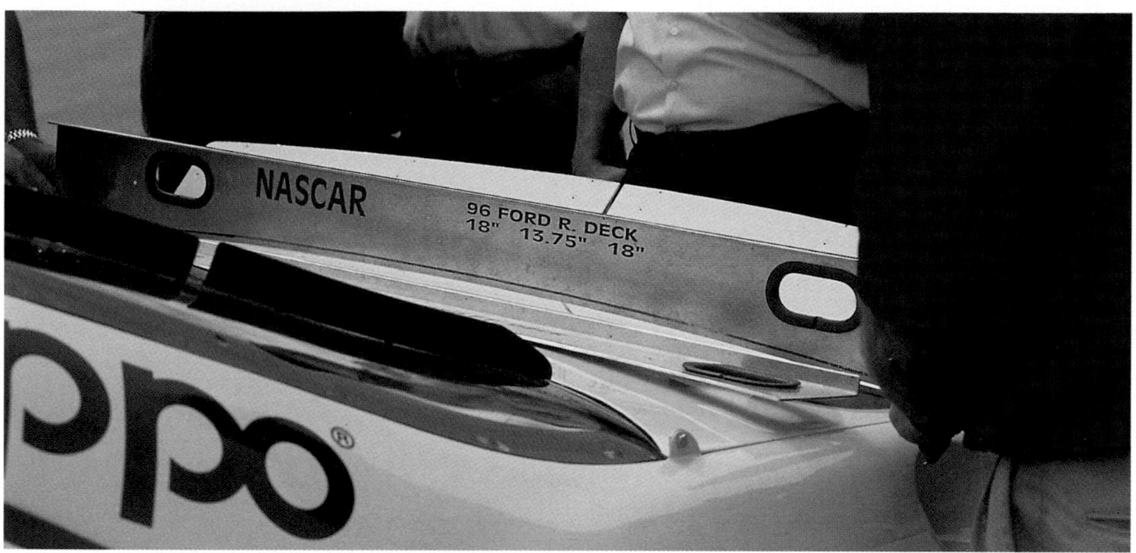


*As many as fifteen templates are used to monitor the shape of each car.*

## --------Round Two

The next round of inspections comes before the first round of qualifying (see chapter 11). Each car, before it attempts to qualify, must complete and pass inspection again.

The top five first-round qualifiers will have their height and weight checked once more before their positions are official.

## --------Round Three

Any car that does not make the field in the first round of qualifying has the opportunity to make a second attempt. First, however... yes, that's right, the car must be inspected again.

After second-round qualifying, the two fastest cars are run through the mill again.

## --------Race Day

Okay. So, both rounds of qualifying are finished, practice sessions are over, shocks, springs, engines, widgets, thingamabobs, doodads all are changed or at least taken apart, looked at by the teams, and put back together. It's now race day, and this is what all the preparation has been for.

But, before the teams are given the okay to push their cars to the starting grid, each and every one of them must—you guessed it—go through NASCAR inspection again.

All of this may seem redundant, but it is necessary to maintain a "level playing field," a fair environment for all teams.

*ABOVE: The goal of NASCAR officials is side-by-side competition between all three car manufacturers. RIGHT: Postrace inspection sometimes begins before the cars even return to the garage. Here officials check spoiler angles after a race.*

## Postrace

The winning team from every NASCAR Winston Cup race can expect the postrace inspection. The car goes through the process of having its height, weight, and so forth checked. Then the winning engine is torn down—completely. The compression ratio and the cubic-inch displacement (see glossary) are checked. Compression ratio in the NASCAR Winston Cup Series is 12.0 to 1 (compared to 9.5 to 1 in the NASCAR Busch Series and NASCAR Craftsman Truck Series). Cubic-inch displacement is a minimum of 350 and maximum of 358 cubic inches.

But this isn't the only engine going through the process. In addition to the winner's car, the pole sitter, the fastest second-round qualifier, the second-place finisher, often the third-place finisher, and one other car picked at random all go through the same postrace inspection process.

## Final Tally

So, for those of you scoring at home: A team is guaranteed to go through a minimum of three inspections and a maximum of six during a race weekend.

CHAPTER THIRTEEN

# DRIVERS' MEETING

## --------Gentlemen, Start the Meeting

Before each race, NASCAR officials meet with the participants to go over some ground rules. Attendance is mandatory for drivers and crew chiefs, but you'll usually find a few team owners, a representative or two from the race sponsor, and maybe a celebrity in the audience as well.

*If a competitor misses the prerace drivers' meeting, he has to start the race at the back of the field.*

PIT STOP *Like we said, this meeting is mandatory for drivers and crew chiefs from each of the teams that are running in the race. If a driver misses the drivers' meeting, he must take the green flag from the rear of the field. Period. If that's not tough enough, if a crew chief misses the meeting, a fine is probable.*

The NASCAR Winston Cup Series race director goes over everything from rules to the location of the green-flag restart line to unique features of the track. He will remind drivers not to impede the progress of the leaders at inappropriate times. That goes hand in hand with one bit of advice that comes up in the meeting every week: *Lapped cars get out of the way late in the race.* And while NASCAR officials do the bulk of the talking at these prerace meetings, it's not unusual for drivers to ask questions or offer words of wisdom on a certain track or situation.

Each week during the drivers' meeting, a minister (from Motor Racing Outreach) leads a prayer giving thanks and asking for a good day for all of those involved. And directly before the race, the minister will hold a chapel service for anyone, specifically the teams and their families, who would like to attend.

PIT STOP *Motor Racing Outreach (MRO) is a ministry that travels with the NASCAR Winston Cup Series. They are at each and every race providing race day prayers and Sunday services for the NASCAR family when they aren't able to attend their regular church services at home.*

*Motor Racing Outreach provides comfort for the entire NASCAR community.*

PART FIVE

# THE MACHINE

BODY AND CHASSIS

THE ENGINE

SETUPS

THE FINISHED PRODUCT

SHOW CARS

CHAPTER FOURTEEN

# 14 BODY AND CHASSIS

When NASCAR got its start in the late 1940s, what is now known as the NASCAR Winston Cup Series was the "Strictly Stock" series, and the cars were just that. Drivers could listen to the radio while they were racing. The "stock" nature of the cars is one of the great allures of NASCAR racing, and it's a fact not lost on the manufacturers and others in the automobile industry, who long ago discovered the truth to the maxim that cars that "win on Sunday sell on Monday."

What sets NASCAR apart from other racing organizations is its commitment to use cars that look just like the ones fans can

find at their local auto dealer. NASCAR has followed this philosophy with unwavering devotion through the years. As a result, the body and "curb appearance" of a NASCAR Winston Cup Chevrolet Monte Carlo, Ford Taurus, and Pontiac Grand Prix look quite similar to their stock counterparts, although if you take a closer look, you'll easily be able to spot the differences.

*OPPOSITE: Every section of a NASCAR race car is carefully crafted to specifications. BELOW: The body of a race car starts as a piece of sheet metal.*

## --------This Is Definitely Not Your Father's Family Sedan

The NASCAR Winston Cup race car is actually sheet metal fabricated around a sturdy frame that includes metal tubing, heavy-duty suspension, roll cage, driver's compartment, fuel cell, and other safety equipment. The showroom car obviously doesn't have any of that racing stuff.

*Every piece of every car centers around the roll cage.*

The reason for the differences is obvious. They are both built to provide maximum safety, but the NASCAR Winston Cup car is also built for speed, while the family sedan is built to provide reliable transportation for several years.

In an effort to maintain a stock appearance for NASCAR Winston Cup cars, NASCAR mandates that certain parts, namely, the grille, hood, bumper panels, and rear deck lid—you probably call it a trunk lid—are identical to those used in production cars. From a distance, the race car and the street car do look similar. In fact, some of the templates NASCAR uses during the inspection process (see chapter 12) would fit the stock body.

But take a closer look. The NASCAR Winston Cup body and chassis also feature:

- A roll cage, designed to protect the driver in accidents.
- A special fuel cell, including a fuel "bladder" that cuts down the risk of fuel spills and fire in accidents.
- Functional front air dam and rear spoiler. Many "sporty" production cars feature spoilers, but if you compare the positioning of the spoiler on the respective cars, you'll see that the production-car spoiler is purely aesthetic.
- A duct, or "cowl," feeding fresh air to the motor compartment for better combustion.
- Much stiffer coil springs both front and rear, which give the race car driver better control and a better "feel" for the track.

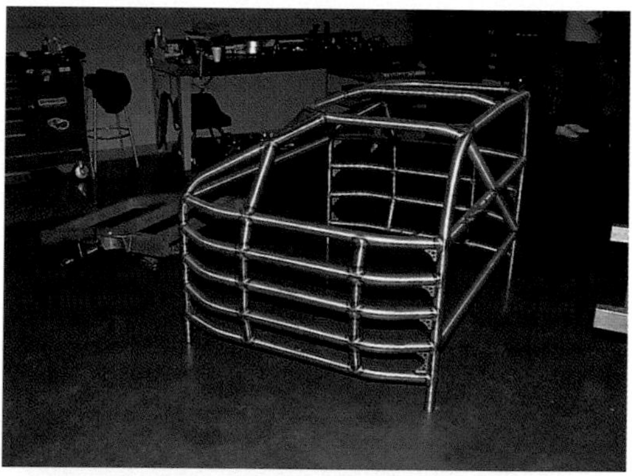

*TOP: Designed to help protect the driver, the bars of a roll cage must meet a specific measurement. MIDDLE: Window nets were developed in the early 1970s. BOTTOM: Which set of springs a team uses is dictated by how the car is handling at each race track.*

- Brake cooling ducts, which channel air to the brake rotors to prevent overheating. That's critical at short tracks such as Martinsville that eat brake systems alive.
- No brake lights or headlights.
- Roof flaps. Two flaps, mounted on the roof of each car and similar to those on the wing of an airplane, deploy during a spin to deflect air and help keep the car on the ground.
- High-performance shocks, which allow teams to adjust air pressure.

The differences don't stop there. The windshield, for example, is installed in three sections. There is no glass in the driver's-side window, but rather a safety net to keep the driver safely in the car. The steering wheel is detachable, allowing the driver easy access. And the hood is fastened down in front by metal pins, which keep it shut at high speeds and allow for quick access.

## Rules, Rules, and More Rules

The rules may change slightly to accommodate different car models each year, but NASCAR Winston Cup cars must generally adhere to several guidelines:

- They must be a NASCAR-approved model made in the current model year or the two previous years.
- Cars must weigh a minimum of 3,400 pounds race-ready (including oil, fuel, and water and not counting the weight of the driver). There is also a weight requirement for the left and right sides of the car, which varies depending on the track.
- The rear spoiler must conform to a maximum height, width, and angle, depending upon the car model.
- The front air dam must have a minimum ground clearance.
- Headlight and parking light openings must be covered.
- Cars must have roof flaps.

There are many more regulations regarding specific parts of the car, down to the smallest detail.

PIT STOP

*Although the Chevrolet Monte Carlo, Pontiac Grand Prix, and Ford Taurus are the predominant cars racing on the NASCAR Winston Cup circuit, several other models are eligible for use. They are the Buick Regal and Oldsmobile Cutlass. Why aren't they used? No team has seriously considered them because those manufacturers just aren't as heavily involved in NASCAR Winston Cup racing. Also, the Ford Thunderbird is eligible for use until the end of 1999.*

CHAPTER FIFTEEN

15

# THE ENGINE

You can talk all you want about the importance of a car's setup, tires, spoilers, whatever, but the engine is the essential element. If a car has a flat tire or not enough "bite" on the track, those problems can be resolved on pit road. Mess up the front-end aerodynamics in an accident? Slap some tape on the car and get it back out there.

You can't put a Band-Aid—or tape—on an engine problem and make it go away. Come up with a bad cylinder? Hey, your chances of a good finish literally just went up in smoke. Blown engine? Go ahead and park the car. Your day is over.

If you don't believe in the importance of the engine, listen to the drivers talk about how vital their team's engine program is. When was the last time you heard a driver mention the spring program, or the spoiler program? Enough said. In fact, the importance of this program is demonstrated by the number of engines each team takes to each race... as many as five.

## Horsepower Galore

When you think about it, comparing a factory production engine and a NASCAR Winston Cup engine would be like comparing the Wright brothers' plane with a modern navy fighter jet. Yes, both utilize the same basic principles, but one is a heck of a lot more efficient. Not to mention faster.

Once again, NASCAR is thorough in detailing to teams what is and isn't allowed in regard to the power plant. In keeping with NASCAR's mission to make NASCAR Winston Cup cars as "stock" as possible, many of the engine specs must be identical with a factory engine, including the number and angle of cylinders, the location of the camshaft, the number of valves per cylinder, the number of intake and exhaust ports, and the location of the spark plugs.

*Engine shops in NASCAR often look like assembly lines.*

*A driver keeps track of how hard his engine is working by reading the tachometer.*

NASCAR also mandates that major components such as the engine block and heads be produced by the manufacturer for sale to the public.

But there are important differences. NASCAR Winston Cup teams use a bushel of high-performance parts designed to generate and withstand high rpm while enduring tough race conditions. Also, whereas new cars today come with a fuel injection system, NASCAR Winston Cup cars still use carburetors. You'll also find few of the things that rob production cars of horsepower.

Bottom line? A NASCAR Winston Cup engine produces over 700 horsepower and can turn 8,600 rpm during a race and as many as 8,900 rpm in qualifying runs. Most street cars are in the 200-horsepower range, and only the highest-performance production cars—such as the Chevrolet Corvette—approach 300 horsepower. And if you tried to push your regular production Ford or Chevy consistently over 5,000 rpm, you'd better have a cell phone handy, to call a tow truck.

PIT STOP

*If you're wondering, these earthshaking machines only get around four miles per gallon, slightly more at the restrictor-plate tracks (Daytona International Speedway and Talladega*

*Superspeedway). With a twenty-two-gallon gas tank, it's no wonder pit stops are such an important part of the sport.*

## Built for Sheer, Unadulterated Speed

Teams use engines specially designed for qualifying. Said engines will have the engine timing advanced, for one thing, and a different carburetor jetting. Other subtle differences, such as a thinner motor oil and transmission fluid—even a different fan blade—enable the car to go as fast as possible for the all-important qualifying lap(s). Qualifying engines are usually built for maximum high-end power, giving the driver the extra jolt needed to rocket down the straight-aways.

After qualifying, the pole-day engine is exchanged for a more durable model, which features better low-end torque. Why is that feature important? Well, the drivers can't run wide open all day. They have to slow down now and then, and when they do, the torque gives them power to pass other cars.

OPPOSITE: Many pieces on a NASCAR stock car engine are the same as those on a passenger car, just bigger. ABOVE: While passenger cars now have fuel-injected engines, NASCAR still uses carburetors.

## Nothing but the Best

While it's true that a few high-performance passenger cars could reach speeds of 150 mph on a race track, their engines would fly apart if such speeds were maintained for any length of time. NASCAR Winston Cup engine builders can, and do, use a wide variety of high-performance aftermarket parts, all designed for workhorse duty.

Special crankshafts, heavy-duty valves and valve springs, connecting rods, distributors, and intake manifolds are just a few of the engine builders' necessities. (If you want to know exactly what brand-name parts they're using, check the contingency decals on the side of the car.)

PIT STOP

*It's not a part of the engine, but every race fan should be familiar with the term "dynamometer." It's a device used to measure an engine's horsepower and test and mon-*

*itor its overall performance. If you really want to impress your friends, you can call it a "dyno" for short.*

## The Fine Print Every Engine Builder Knows by Heart

Currently, teams must use a V-8 "small-block" engine with a displacement of between 350 and 358 cubic inches in size. NASCAR officials can tell if a car is even one-half inch over the size limit. Of course, the engine size of the winner and other top finishers is checked after each race.

NASCAR regulates a few other engine particulars, including:

- The engine block used to start a race must be used throughout the entire race.
- No aluminum blocks are permitted.
- All engine oil pans and engine oil coolers must be approved by NASCAR.
- There is a minimum ground clearance.

*Teams often change engines between qualifying and the race.*

*Engine builders often "tweak" the ignition timing a couple of degrees.*

The NASCAR rule book spells out in minute detail what is, and isn't, allowed in regard to the engine. For example, Section 20-5.1 specifies that "Engines in all eligible makes and models cannot be located further back than the centerline of the forward most spark plug hole on the right side cylinder head in line with the upper ball joint."

There you have it. Any questions?

NASCAR's rigid guidelines for what can go into the engine compartment serve a purpose. They help ensure competitors use stock parts where applicable. Also, by prohibiting illegal or unapproved parts, NASCAR helps maintain a level playing field. In an area where even the slightest change—such as the size of the oil pan—can mean a big edge in performance, NASCAR is simply covering all the bases.

## What the Engine Builder Giveth, NASCAR Can Taketh Away

Another method engine builders use to tweak extra power out of an engine is by advancing the ignition timing a couple of degrees. This creates a more lasting spark, which makes for better combus-

Even the smallest parts of each engine are checked thoroughly before they go into the car.

tion. It also gives the cars that distinctive "thumpita-thumpita-thumpita" sound that literally makes the ground rumble even when a car is idling. (Not having any muffler system adds to the effect.)

Engine builders make their living finding ways to produce more speed. Unfortunately, they often become victims of their own success. When cars began routinely breaking the 200-mph barrier at Daytona and Talladega, NASCAR gave the engine builders restrictor plates to work with. Now, as speeds are creeping up at other tracks, NASCAR has made other changes. Designed to cut horsepower and enhance competition by slowing speeds, NASCAR has mandated a lower engine compression ratio beginning in 1998. That ratio, which measures the pressure under which the fuel mixture burns in the cylinder, was reduced from 14.0:1 to 12.0:1.

PIT STOP

*Restrictor plates are flat metal devices used to reduce the airflow into the carburetor. The mixture of air and fuel creates horsepower. The reduction of that mixture therefore cuts horsepower and speeds.*

*According to some engine builders, that should knock off ten to twelve units of horsepower. But if history holds true to form, the engine builders will find a way to get it back over time.*

## The Ri$ing Co$t of Hor$epower

No one said building a race-ready NASCAR Winston Cup engine was cheap. One single engine will cost a race team anywhere from $40,000 to $50,000, and that cost has risen dramatically in recent years. And as any race fan can tell you, these finely tuned works of engineering can become ruined blocks of scrap metal in the space of a lap.

That cost, of course, does not include the expense of in-house engine builders and associated costs like research and development. The price of speed at NASCAR's highest level is enough to shock even racing veterans these days. A change in philosophy is partly to blame. In the early days of the sport, drivers would use the same engine until it literally wouldn't run anymore. Even a few years ago, teams used some parts, such as rods and bearings, for two or three races.

Now teams use basically brand-new engines each race. You're talking forty-two engines right there. Then, you need roughly half that many qualifying engines, as well as a handful of engines to use in test sessions.

CHAPTER SIXTEEN

# 16 SETUPS

## It's a Setup

Watch a race on TV, and before the first two laps have been run, the announcers will start talking about the "setup" of a particular car or cars. Given the parity in competition today, a car's setup can literally mean the difference between winning and finishing twenty cars back.

The setup refers to the adjustments made to a car to help it handle on the track. Tire pressure is an element of the setup, as are the shocks, springs, weight distribution, and aerodynamics.

Not surprisingly, the setup differs from track to track. No matter how good a team's car is at Bristol, for example, the same setup would fail to make the field at Talladega. The short-track car is set up for frequent braking and responsive cornering while at a superspeedway the drivers stand on the gas all day long. With the wide racing groove there, cornering is less of a concern.

PIT STOP

*While setups differ greatly from a short track to a superspeedway, the teams are also working with entirely different cars. Most teams have many different cars built for the various tracks on the circuit, be it a road-course car for Watkins Glen, a short-track racer for Bristol, a flat-track car for Dover, an intermediate speedway car for Atlanta, or a superspeedway rocket for Daytona. So comparing the setups between the tracks is tough when, in reality, you*

*A car is placed on jack stands to make work on the suspension easier.*

*have entirely different cars to handle each assignment.*

*In a nutshell, though, short-track cars are built and set up with an emphasis on handling. Superspeedway cars are set up with aerodynamics in mind.*

## Boys, All We Need Is One Good Lap

As with the engine, each car's setup is different for qualifying. Crew chiefs usually have a good idea of the necessary changes, but often their car requires a completely different setup than in the last visit to the track, depending upon the weather and track conditions.

Drivers offer constant feedback during practice so changes can be made if necessary. But generally speaking, crew chiefs will set their cars up to run with stiffer springs and shocks. Spring rubbers, which are tiny pieces of rubber, can be added or taken out of the springs to improve the car's

*Shocks are a key when trying to get a car just right for a driver.*

*The better a car handles, the easier a driver can be on the brakes.*

response and handling. The crew will add a little more air pressure in the tires to help the tires heat up quicker because warm tires are faster.

Sometimes, even a simple change can make a difference. For example, since an overheated engine is not a problem for a one- or two-lap qualifying run, crew members will tape up a car's grille and air intake ducts with ordinary household duct tape to decrease the airflow entering through the grille, which, in turn, makes the car more aerodynamic. That may mean only fractions of a second in speed, but that can be an eternity in NASCAR Winston Cup qualifying.

**PIT STOP**

*You'll often hear race announcers or crew chiefs talking about a certain team adding—or taking out—a "round of wedge" or a "round of bite" to their car. This refers to the turning or adjusting of a car's jacking screws found at each wheel. This redistributes the car's weight at each wheel, depending on which screw(s) is turned. If you've watched even one race, you've proba-*

*bly noticed a crewman with a long ratchet-type wrench plug into a hole in the back of the car to adjust the bite.*

*These changes can help correct a "loose" car (a car that feels like the rear wheels are going to spin out in turns) as well as a "tight" car, a situation where the front wheels don't want to behave.*

## There's Rarely Any Suspense When It Comes to the Suspension

The suspension components are not the most glamorous parts on a race car, but they serve an important purpose: They help stabilize the car on the track.

The suspension really should get more credit. After all, suspension parts hold the wheels on the car. But they never get any praise for a good run. When a member of the suspension team finally does get noticed, it's usually something along the lines of, "Oh, no, looks like the number 83 car has lost its rear sway bar. Tough break there."

But that's just the way it is. These parts do tend to go unnoticed until something goes wrong. Major components of the suspension include:

- The front and rear coil springs, which support the weight of the car and are critical to the "feel" of the car. Crews can add or subtract spring rubbers to adjust the ride.
- Front and rear sway bars, which help keep the car from excessive leaning in the turns.
- Shock absorbers, which are pretty self-explanatory. Teams use heavy-duty shocks, which can be adjusted to change the ride.
- Upper and lower A-frames. These parts are attached to the frame at one end. The spindles are attached at the

*Tools of the trade.*

*To make a certain spring feel just right, spring rubbers are often used to improve a car's handling.*

other end. The wheels and brake rotors are attached to the spindles. (Confused? Try this little reminder: The A-frame bone's connected to the spindle-bone, the spindle-bone's connected to the...)

- Spindles, wheel bearings, and hubs. Simply put, they hold the wheels on the car and allow them to turn freely.

## The Wind in Their Sails (and on Their Trunk Lids)

Spoilers are metal strips that help control airflow and downforce and to make the car more aerodynamic. The front spoiler, or "air dam," is underneath the car's front end, while the rear spoiler is attached to the trunk lid. These pieces must adhere to minimum height and width requirements and must be nonadjustable. Before NASCAR put in the "nonadjustable" requirement a couple of years ago, teams could improve their cornering ability by "adding more spoiler," or increasing the rear spoiler's angle in relation to the rear window. If need be, the spoiler angle could be decreased to improve straight-away speed.

Without spoilers, it would be impossible for the drivers to run the speeds they run, especially at the faster tracks. Spoilers have been a very highly publicized side of the race setup in the last couple of years. Even

*The angle of the rear spoiler on a car can change handling dramatically.*

a quarter-inch change in height can make a huge difference in stability at racing speeds.

## --------Gearing It Up

The role of rear-end gearing in a car's performance is often overlooked by fans. Crew chiefs do so at their own peril. Say, for example, you've got two cars running door to door out of the final turn at Bristol Motor Speedway. One car suddenly bolts past the other into the lead and goes on to take the checkered flag.

It could be the winning driver had a stronger engine, or more skill. Then again, he might have had a better rear-end gear for the situation. Simply put, the rear-end gearing helps translate the car's power to the rear wheels. It is expressed in ratios, such as 2.92 to 1 (meaning the pinion will turn 2.92 times for each turn by the ring gear).

Track size is the most important variable in choosing a rear-end gear. For example, a smaller track like Martinsville would call for a ratio something along the lines of 6.20 to 1, while superspeedways such as Talladega and Daytona would be closer to a 3-to-1 ratio. Other factors teams consider when picking a gear are weather and the engine specs.

As you might expect, teams also go with a different gear in qualifying, often using a higher gear ratio to help the driver keep his rpm up in the corners.

The engine builder usually has a lot of input in this area, because he knows at which rpm range his motor can reach peak performance. Picking the correct rear-end gear is an important part of that setup. Choose the wrong gear and you can end up with a blown engine. Make a wrong decision the other way and the driver won't be able to keep his engine rpm up going into and coming out of the corners. And that can be the difference between winning and losing.

Most drivers have their own preference in rear-end gearing, with most opting for a lower gear (i.e., a higher ratio) for better acceleration out of the corners. Unfortunately for the drivers, few get much input into which gear to run.

PIT STOP

*When talking gear ratios, it helps to remember that the higher the ratio, the "shorter" the gear. Also, a car with a higher ratio will have better acceleration, but a lower top-end speed. The opposite is true with a lower, or "taller," gear ratio.*

CHAPTER SEVENTEEN

17

# THE FINISHED PRODUCT

When fans settle down in their seats at the race track—or in front of the TV—to watch a NASCAR Winston Cup Series race, what they don't see is the hundreds of hours of testing, engine building, and paint and bodywork that go into putting a car in the starting grid on race day. They don't see the man-hours spent behind the scenes. Dropping the engine in the car. Towing the show car down back roads across the country. All-day test sessions at a track five hundred miles from home during what is supposed to be an "off week."

It's no secret that eighteen-hour days are part of the sport at this level. But when the green flag drops on Sunday, all the hassles are quickly forgotten as the sights and sounds of racing fill the air. This is what the team has worked so hard for all week and what makes it all worthwhile.

Monday, it's back to work until finally, the next weekend, Nirvana arrives again.

## Hoist Away, Mateys

A NASCAR Winston Cup team can put a new engine in their car in about an hour, roughly half that time in an emergency situation. That's pretty quick, but then again, these guys get lots of practice, possibly making several engine changes each week between the testing, qualifying, and race engines.

Using an engine hoist, it takes about six men to guide the power plant into the engine compartment, bolt it down, bolt on the transmission, and attach all the requisite hoses, clamps, wires.

## Safety First and Foremost

Going 190 mph around the race track in a tight group is a big part of the allure of NASCAR. Unfortunately, such situations also pose the potential for accidents at literally every turn.

Injuries are a part of any sport, and racing is no exception. But from the beginning of NASCAR a half century ago, safety has been of the utmost concern. In fact, much of the NASCAR rule book is filled with recommendations to enhance safety. For example, several pages cover guidelines regarding just the fuel system and the handling of fuel in the pits.

NASCAR also specifies that:

*Teams can change an engine in about an hour.*

- Drivers have a quick-release lap belt and a shoulder harness no less than three inches wide.
- There are padded rib protectors and seat leg extensions on both sides of the driver's seat.
- The seat has a padded headrest.
- Roll bars must be made of steel, not aluminum, and any bars within reach of the driver must be padded.

New safety innovations come along on a regular basis. In the 1960s, the inner-liner tire—which is basically a tire-within-a-tire—was developed, protecting drivers from losing control when they cut a tire. Later, a specially designed fuel bladder cut down on the risk of fire in accidents in which the fuel tank is ruptured.

Drivers help their own cause by wearing safety helmets and fireproof uniforms, gloves, and boots. Each car also must carry an onboard fire extinguisher.

It may be hard to believe, but as recently as the 1960s, drivers drove five-hundred-mile races on superspeedways clad in nothing more than jeans, loafers, and a T-shirt. Whoever said that things were better in the old days?

PIT STOP

*The history of NASCAR has seen many accidents that have led directly to safety devices designed to prevent injuries in such future accidents. For example, after a series of accidents at superspeedways in the late*

*ABOVE: Head socks provide added protection under a helmet. BELOW: Quick-release belts and shoulder harnesses have evolved after years of testing.*

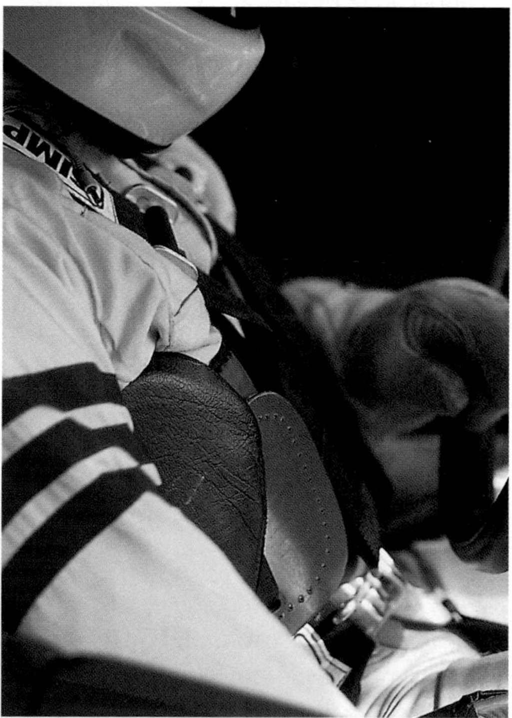

*1980s in which cars became airborne, Roush Industries, in conjunction with Embry-Riddle Aeronautical University in Daytona Beach, Florida, General Motors, Ford, and NASCAR, developed roof flaps. Located at the rear of the roof line, the flaps pop up when a car spins around, keeping the car from taking flight. Going further back, an accident involving NASCAR legend Richard Petty resulted in the development of the driver safety net in the driver's-side window.*

*Safety innovations aren't limited to the cars. Helmets, drivers' suits, even the retaining walls and catch fences at race tracks have all been refined through the years to provide the maximum in protection for drivers and fans. Rules such as the pit road speed limit and NASCAR penalties for sloppy pit work (loose tires on pit road, etc.) have increased safety for pit workers as well.*

*Form-fitting seats offer padded rib protectors and seat-leg extensions.*

## Everyone Needs a Backup Plan

Teams take two cars to each race track, the primary car and a backup car, which stays on the trailer. (Occasionally, a low-budget team will have to go home after wrecking its primary car, because they don't have a backup.) However, the backup car can't be pulled out at will and substituted for the primary car, no matter how bad the primary car is running. The backup can only be swapped for a car that has been wrecked beyond repair, a determination that must be made by the NASCAR Winston Cup Series director.

NASCAR's rules on this are quite strict. In fact, the backup car can't even be unloaded off the race hauler without NASCAR's approval.

## Our Sponsor Wants a Pink Car with Purple Polka Dots?

Corporate sponsors pay big-time money (as much as $6 million per year) for the privilege of putting their corporate logo and colors on a race car. So you better believe the sponsor is going to get the logo and colors it wants on the car. But the sponsor doesn't take these decisions lightly. With so much money on the line, the company wants to get the maximum return on its investment. If they don't have the in-house design staff to do the job, most major sponsors now hire outside firms to come up with a logo and color scheme that will show off their cars. There are a number of important decisions to make: What colors to use? Is the sponsor's logo visible for both television viewers and fans at the race track? Which part of their product line are they advertising, and how can they best reach hard-core as well as casual racing fans?

Finding the right combination for all these variables isn't easy. Each race features cars indistinguishable to both fans at the race track and TV viewers, cars that make you squint hard before asking your friend beside you, "Who's that sponsoring that car?" But there are plenty of success stories. Who hasn't come to associate Dale Jarrett with the red, white, and blue Ford Quality Care car? Or Jeff Gordon with the DuPont rainbow Chevrolet? Or Dale Earnhardt with the black GM Goodwrench Service Plus Chevrolet? Of course, running in the top five week in and week out, as the aforementioned drivers do, definitely helps sponsor recognition.

Almost without exception, the primary sponsor on the car determines what it looks like.

PIT STOP

*The pink car reference is only a slight exaggeration. Early in his career, seven-time NASCAR Winston Cup champion Dale Earnhardt, the infamous "Man in Black," was "Pretty in Pink" as he drove a pink race car.*

## The Color of Money

Painting and decaling a NASCAR Winston Cup car is an expensive, time-consuming process. But it's a necessary part of the business, as race fans—and the sponsors—pay good money to see their favorite driver in a shiny, spotless car each race weekend. Therefore, most NASCAR Winston Cup teams have a couple of paint and body workers on staff.

*Speaking of pink, Exide Batteries chose it.*

Typically, it takes about three days from start to finish to paint and decal a car, at a cost of around $3,000. The work goes something like this: First the bare sheet metal must be cleaned, as even the slightest dirt, dust, or debris will cause imperfections in the paint. Next, the car is surfaced with Bondo, then block-sanded and pretaped. The car is then sprayed with primer—it helps the paint adhere to the body. After that, the car must be sanded and taped again, before it's finally ready to paint. Once it's painted the car must sit for about forty-eight hours for the paint to cure before the decals can be applied.

The paint and body guys on a team must cringe when their driver "swaps paint" with another car.

PIT STOP

*Adding even more cost to the paint game is the proliferation in recent years of special "commemorative" cars, special paint schemes designed to celebrate special occasions for drivers or their sponsors. Paint and body men might grumble about the extra work involved, but the special paint schemes have proved tremendously popular with fans, sponsors, and collectors of die-cast cars and other memorabilia.*

## Testing, Testing, One-Two-Three

Testing is a critical part of NASCAR Winston Cup racing today. Teams squeeze testing in whenever the schedule allows—before the season, right after a race, during an off week, and so on.

What they hope to accomplish depends on their situation. Some teams with new drivers show up to give the new guy an idea of what to expect when he next visits the track. Other teams go to test a new car or a different setup, to check fuel mileage for pit stop strategy, and the like.

The teams are limited to seven tests each season, with each test to consist of not more than three days in a row at any single track. Yet even with the limited testing dates, some drivers have difficulty finding time to participate, given their demanding personal appearance schedules. As a result, some teams hire drivers—even other NASCAR Winston Cup drivers—to test their equipment.

*As soon as a car is painted, sponsor decals are applied.*

PIT STOP

*Citing the skyrocketing costs involved with fielding a NASCAR Winston Cup team, some in the racing community have called for an end to testing. When you add up the costs for testing, such as for tires, meals and lodging, and track rentals—which can cost $1,500 to $5,000 per day, depending on the track—testing might seem like a waste of money to some team owners. But while they bemoan the costs, team owners don't complain too loudly when the results of one of their tests put their car in victory lane.*

CHAPTER EIGHTEEN

18

# SHOW CARS

## --------Showin' Off

One of the driving forces behind NASCAR's explosive growth in popularity in recent years has been the interaction between drivers and fans. Drivers are far more accessible to the fans than the athletes in other sports, and are usually happy to oblige a fan for an autograph or photo.

But a driver, being only one person, can only be one place at any given time. A team's show cars, on the other hand, can

*After actual race cars are built and raced, they are often "retired" as show cars.*

travel across the country, taking the sport to the fans where they live, work, and play.

Some teams have several cars and a couple of employees on staff whose main duty is to haul the show cars by trailer from site to site. These guys can be on the road more than two hundred days a year, logging sixty thousand miles or more. It's an expensive operation, meaning that some of the smaller, single-car operations can't afford a show car.

It's worth noting that many major sponsors buy their own show cars and take it upon themselves to tow the cars around and set them up for promotional opportunities.

## Say, That Looks Just Like a Real Race Car

If show cars look just like the "real thing," that's entirely by design. They are real race cars, with engines, safety equipment, a roll cage, and other features just as you'd find them on a car at the track. Often, show cars are race cars that are no longer useful for racing. With a little bodywork, they look perfect sitting out in front of your local grocery store. Other show cars are race cars that for one reason or another are no longer competitive. Rather than relegate them to the scrap pile, the teams convert them to the show-car circuit.

## NASCAR Winston Cup Racing at Your Local Supermarket (or Hardware Store, or Shopping Mall)

You'll find show cars just about anywhere you could expect to find NASCAR fans—outside the race track, at the local supermarket or auto parts store, you name it.

Why have a show car?

A better question might be, why not? Show cars spread goodwill for the race team and its sponsor, which down the line might translate into new fans purchasing that driver's souvenirs, or that sponsor's detergent or motor oil. In fact, many sponsor agreements with teams outline the number of appearances expected by a show car and so forth. Sponsors can tie in the appearance of a show car with an in-store promotion and almost guarantee a huge response.

In short, show cars are a win-win situation for the drivers, teams, sponsors, and the fans.

*Even Daytona USA, the official attraction of NASCAR, has its own show car.*

PART SIX

# AT THE TRACK

THE TRACKS

ETIQUETTE

SOUVENIRS

CHAPTER NINETEEN

19

# THE TRACKS

By the time you get to the speedway for qualifying and, of course, race day, the place is buzzing right along. From your spot in the grandstands, it looks like there are thousands of people on the "other side of the fence." Well, by the time the starter gets ready to wave the green flag, several thousand souls are in the pits and garage. So, who bosses this mass of humanity in the stands, infield, and competition area?

It's really simple. Speedway personnel are in charge of advertising the event, selling tickets, and providing parking and customer amenities. That's making sure that

once you've purchased a ticket, your seat is ready for you and not occupied by someone else. It also means it's up to the track to see you're not hassled by somebody who doesn't like your driver.

**PIT STOP**

*Traffic control is critical at most tracks. State and local police are in charge of traffic on highways leading into and out of the track. The speedway's own security forces take over once traffic enters the speedway grounds. Also, track security is responsible for your safety, but guards may call upon the police when needed.*

*NASCAR controls the pits and garage, and its personnel are responsible for conducting the race. The NASCAR officials who are visible to you are the flagman, pace car driver, and inspectors in the pits. But they all take their orders from the NASCAR Winston Cup Series director and other officials who are tucked away in the control tower.*

*If you purchase a ticket, your seat will be waiting for you.*

## What Kind of Track Is This?

Basically, the NASCAR Winston Cup Series races on three types of tracks—road courses, short tracks, and superspeedways. A road course is a closed course with lots of left- and right-hand turns, as well as short and long straightaways. Traditionally, all road races are conducted in a clockwise direction.

A short track is an oval that's less than one mile around, and a superspeedway is anything that's a mile or more in distance. For statistical purposes, NASCAR lumps road courses in with superspeedways. Just as no one seems to know why road racers go from right to left, nobody can explain why oval track racers have always "turned left." Some say it's because early races were run on horse tracks, which customarily ran counterclockwise.

PIT STOP

*The competitors use these terms a bit differently because they think in terms of chassis science and engine horsepower. To a driver, a short track is still anything less than a mile. An "intermediate" track is anything from a mile to a mile and a half, while a "speedway" is two miles or longer.*

*At two and a half miles long, Daytona International Speedway is considered a superspeedway.*

## What Do I Need at the Track?

For our purposes, there are two main areas for race fans to view a race: the infield and the grandstands. If you're among the first group, we really don't need to tell you what to bring to a race. Whether you arrive in a top-of-the-line motor home, a travel trailer, a converted school bus, or your cousin's '65 Ford pickup with a couple of pup tents, you will need to bring everything necessary for survival.

This is directed at the latter group—the fans in the grandstands. First, you'll want to dress properly. If you absolutely know it's going to be a hot, humid day, do not bring your parka or winter jacket. On the other hand, if you're expecting a chill in the air, dress warmly and bring a blanket, cap, and gloves. In other words, check the weather forecast before you leave home (which is always available on NASCAR Online—www.nascar.com)!

*OPPOSITE: In 1997, 6,091,356 fans attended NASCAR Winston Cup races. BELOW: Camping in the infield is one of the most popular ways to watch a NASCAR race.*

Other items include (and we may have forgotten something): a seat cushion, sunblock, sunglasses, a cap or at least a visor, binoculars, earplugs, portable radio, scanner with a list of driver frequencies, some sort of "tarp" or rain gear if you suspect wet weather, AND a cooler, if permitted by the race track.

A word about this important item. Most speedways do not allow coolers more than fourteen inches long, and track personnel check them for glass containers. So it's okay to bring canned beverages, but glass is forbidden. And as far as food goes, hey, whatever turns you on!

*Best friends don't always agree on who they think is the best driver.*

## Who Are Those Cats?

There is also another type of race fan that we'll call...the "suite-heart." Did you ever wonder who gets to go into all those VIP suites above you while you're packed in with the proletariat? They can be just about anybody—executives of sponsoring companies, their friends, friends of friends and customers, even regular race fans.

Consider a contingency award sponsor (see chapter 9). It may lease a suite for a season to entertain its distributors, retailers, and potential customers. In reality, anyone with enough money—even you—can rent a suite. Some tracks have deals where you can rent part of a suite. Charlotte Motor Speedway pioneered the "speedway club" concept. They sell individual seats in suites to folks who may just want to sit in a suite and be able to eat, drink, and be merry without having to lay out thousands of dollars for a whole suite that seats sixty-four.

*Some would consider this the best seat in the house.*

CHAPTER TWENTY

20

# ETIQUETTE

## In the Grandstands—Be Nice Now!

Etiquette is just a fancy word for accepted rules of behavior in a certain place or situation. Race-watching is supposed to be fun, and you have every right to enjoy yourself. Sure, go ahead and whoop, holler, and stand up. Everybody else does. When your driver is leading, yell, cheer, and give him the ol' high five.

But if your boy's having a rough day, don't take it out on the guy next to you,

*Whoop and holler and, well, just be courteous.*

who may be cheering for somebody you don't like. He's there to have fun, too, and his idea of fun isn't having you describe his driver in terms that would make a construction worker blush.

PIT STOP

*Just a word about throwing things. DON'T! Not only will you be thrown out of the track and quite possibly arrested but debris on the track is extremely dangerous to the drivers.*

## In the Garage—Watch Where You're Walking

If you're fortunate enough to latch on to a garage pass, there are a few rules you must follow. One, dress appropriately. That means no open-toe sandals, cutoffs, shorts, and tank tops. Alcoholic beverages are also prohibited. If you're part of a garage tour, stay with the group leader and watch where you walk because, like speedometers and fuel gauges, NASCAR race cars do not have horns! Remember, it *is* a garage.

*When you're in the pit and garage areas, remember the rules.*

PIT STOP

*A word about autographs. Almost no driver, crew chief, or other team member will refuse to give you a signature, but NASCAR frowns on autograph hounds in the garage area. Why? Well, the guys are there to work and are thinking about one thing only—the race.*

CHAPTER TWENTY-ONE

# 21 SOUVENIRS

It's hard to believe that about twenty years ago if a race fan wanted a souvenir, he'd have to go to a baseball game. Well, maybe it wasn't that extreme, but the racing souvenir and apparel business has really exploded in the past ten or fifteen years.

This is especially evident at the race track. There are literally rows and rows of souvenir trailers, and almost every driver, team, sponsor, and car make is represented. Caps, jackets, T-shirts, pullovers, watches, drinking glasses, posters, race cards . . . there's tons of stuff to buy. You can spend

*ABOVE: Everyone is looking for official souvenirs at the track. LEFT: Fans line up to get a look at a driver's newest item.*

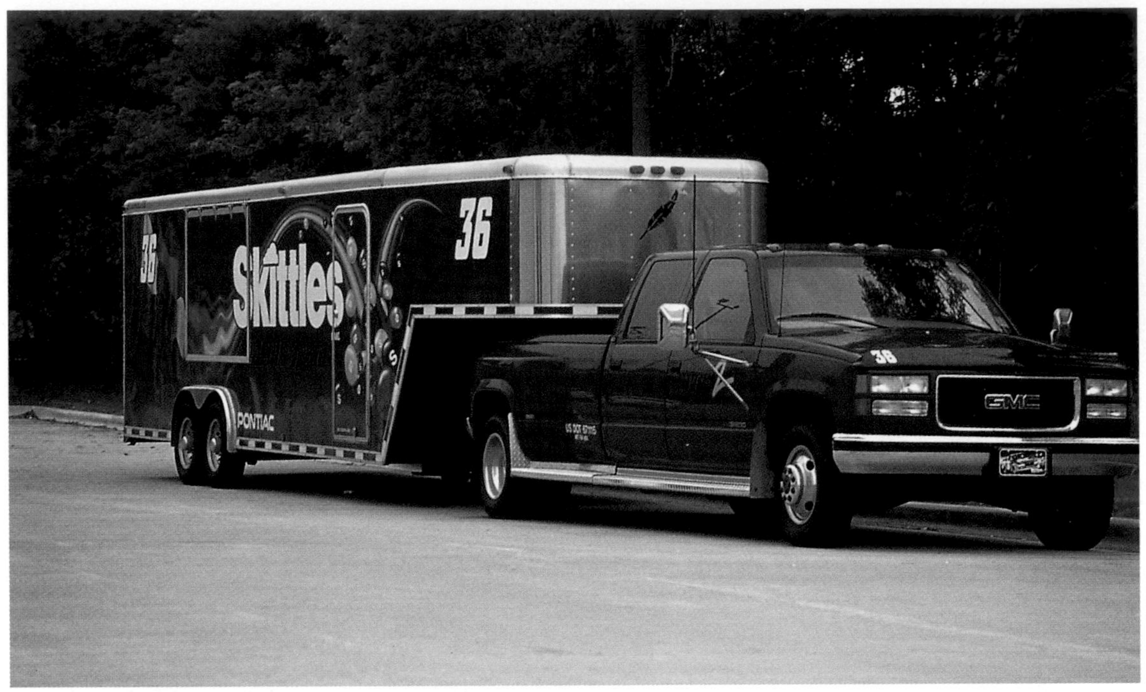


*Souvenir trailers travel as much as the teams do.*

as little as five bucks or more than several hundred depending on the item.

Is there a lot of money to be made from souvenirs? Here's an example: A few years ago it was said that for every dollar Dale Earnhardt made on the race track, he made ten more off it! Not every driver is as successful and popular as Earnhardt, but you get the point.

One thing's for sure, though. If a driver's line of stuff isn't officially licensed or endorsed by him, it's probably a bootleg. What's the problem here? Simple: If it's bootleg it's probably junk and won't last. Who wants to buy merchandise that isn't authentic anyway?!

PART SEVEN

# WHEN THE CHECKERED FLAG DROPS

CHAPTER TWENTY-TWO

# 22 THE FINISH

The car running first completes the last lap, flashes under the checkered flag, and the race is over. While everyone else starts packing up and all the losing drivers bring their cars back to the garage area, the winner and his team head for victory lane—after a victory lap, of course.

So do a lot of other people. Who are they? you ask. Well, first you have the photographers snapping away, trying to get *the* picture. The television network broadcasting the event is there and has "first rights" to the driver. They will either interview him before he has a chance to exit his car and

*ABOVE: What every driver races for—to take the checkers first. OPPOSITE: "How does it feel?" The media immediately wants to talk to the winner.*

acknowledge his win or wait until he gets out of the car and does a little celebrating first. The choice usually depends on the network and how much time is left in the broadcast.

Whichever the case, when the driver climbs out of the car, he usually heads to its roof, waves to the crowd, jumps down, hugs his wife, drinks some champagne. Then it's the radio network's turn for an interview. Usually at least one local television station is also in victory lane, so they'll get their interview.

Once television and radio get what they need, the driver faces the photo corps and begins the traditional "hat dance." Each hat he puts on represents a company that had something to do with providing the driver with the ever-important money he and his team need to race. There may be up to a dozen different hats along with a dozen different photos. Every "hat shot" is recorded by the photographers. It may seem like bedlam, but a driver who just won a NASCAR Winston Cup race doesn't mind, and each photo is very worthwhile for the sponsors.

## It's an Official Race...When?

It doesn't matter if a race is three hundred laps, four hundred miles, whatever. Once the halfway point is reached, the event becomes "official." If it starts raining, snowing, or what have you after a race is half over and if there's no possible way to continue, the race can be considered officially completed.

But that doesn't happen very often. A race is normally over when, according to NASCAR, the "advertised distance" has been completed. That simply means that a race is over when the leading driver finishes all five hundred miles. But what happens if a driver who is running first and has lapped everybody else three times is in an accident on his final lap? Then the guy in second, in order to win, has to keep going until he completes the advertised distance.

*ABOVE: A race is official at the halfway point but isn't over until the leader takes the checkered flag. OPPOSITE: The thrill of victory.*

It doesn't matter how many laps everyone else makes. The race is over when the leader goes the number of laps or miles the promoter promised he'd give you.

PIT STOP

*As we mentioned in chapter 12, victory doesn't come without a few extra responsibilities. Remember, a few cars must be inspected one final time once the race is completed. Usually five cars are chosen (there's a minimum of three) including the winner, the pole sitter, the second- and third-place finishers, and one other randomly picked car. No fudging allowed!*

GM
Goodwrench
Service Plus
AC Delco
AC Delco
AC Delco
AC Delco
NASCAR
RACE CAR
NASCAR
Winston Cup
BUSCH
BEER
Pole Award
HURST
SHIFTERS
Gatorade
Goody's
HEADACHE POWDERS
CARBS
CLEVITE
ENGINE PARTS
Auto Meter
Stant
RADIATOR PRESSURE CAPS
3M
Mechanix
JESEL
3
Goo
Servic
Snap-on
GM

CHAPTER TWENTY-THREE

# GOING HOME

## Adios... Until Next Week

Once the winner has given his final interview and the inspectors have finished their work, the race is over, *really*. For the drivers, it's a trip home for a day or so—unless there's some kind of commitment between then and the next event. Many of the drivers have their own motor homes, so if home is not too far from the speedway,

*OPPOSITE: One of the trickiest parts of leaving a race track is getting out.*

STANLEY
NASCAR BUSCH SERIES
ROYAL OAK
Bud

they use them to travel. If it is a long-distance haul, though, a lot of the teams and drivers have private planes, which makes all the constant traveling a lot easier. Others may choose a commercial flight or may just get into a car and motor away.

The crew member that always uses the highways, at least thirty-three times a year, is the driver of the team hauler. Once the truck is loaded with cars, parts, and other things needed to run a race, he usually tries to get out of the track as soon as he can. In most cases, it's a long way back to the shop. And once he gets there, it's his responsibility to see that the truck is unloaded, cleaned, checked, and then restocked for the next race. The same routine is usually followed by NASCAR officials and inspectors. They leave the track as soon as possible and prepare for the following race.

The team hauler has to be at the gate as soon as the track gates open on the first day of the event (usually by 6:00 A.M.). The crewmen who are essential in making sure the car is ready for the driver have to be at the gate too. Their day usually ends at 5:00 P.M. when NASCAR issues the command, "The garage is closed!"

Many teams take advantage of what they call the "Race Day Express." Many pit crew members don't have to be at the race track until race day to service the car. Instead of paying for food and expensive hotels for his pit crew members, a team owner will fly them in on race day and send them off when the race is over.

*Loading up after the race.*

Usually, the driver won't show up until the day of first-round qualifying. If it's a Sunday race, time trials are, most of the time, held Friday afternoon. Between races drivers take care of things like TV appearances, autograph sessions, sponsor commitments, and sometimes test sessions at other tracks.

In fact, many drivers will flat-out tell you the time they most look forward to is Sunday afternoon. They can get into the car, get a few minutes of peace and quiet, and prepare to do their jobs.

# A HANDY DIRECTORY

*Fans need to keep track of their favorite drivers and where they're racing next.*

Want to know where the track is located? Want to know how to contact a television station that broadcasts NASCAR Winston Cup races? How about a radio network? Here's a handy directory that contains track, TV, radio, and other organizational information you should find useful:

## NASCAR Winston Cup Tracks

**Atlanta Motor Speedway**
P.O. Box 500
Hampton, GA 30228
Tickets: (770) 946-4211
Information: (770) 946-3950

**Bristol Motor Speedway**
P.O. Box 3966
Bristol, TN 37625
Tickets: (423) 764-1161
Information: (423) 764-3534

**California Speedway**
9300 Cherry Ave.
Fontana, CA 92335
Tickets: 800-944-RACE
Information: (909) 429-5000

**Charlotte Motor Speedway**
P.O. Box 600
Concord, NC 28026-0600
Tickets: (704) 455-3200
Information: (704) 455-3209

**Darlington Raceway**
P.O. Box 500
Darlington, SC 29532
Tickets: (803) 395-8499
Information: (803) 395-8892

**Daytona International Speedway**
P.O. Box 2801
Daytona Beach, FL 32120-2801
Tickets: (904) 253-7223
Information: (904) 947-6800

**Dover Downs International Speedway**
P.O. Box 843
Dover, DE 19903
Tickets: 800-441-RACE
Information: (302) 674-4600

**Indianapolis Motor Speedway**
P.O. Box 24910
Speedway, IN 46224
Tickets: 800-822-4639
Information: (317) 484-6780

**Las Vegas Motor Speedway**
7000 Las Vegas Blvd. N.
Las Vegas, NV 89115
Tickets: (702) 644-4443
Information: (702) 644-4444

**Martinsville Speedway**
P.O. Box 3311
Martinsville, VA 24115-3311
Tickets: (540) 956-3151
Information: (540) 956-1600

**Michigan Speedway**
12626 U.S. 12
Brooklyn, MI 49230-9058
Tickets: 800-354-1010
Information: (517) 592-6671

**New Hampshire International Speedway**
P.O. Box 7888
Loudon, NH 03301
Tickets & Information: (603) 783-4931

**North Carolina Speedway**
P.O. Box 500
Rockingham, NC 28379
Tickets: (910) 582-2861
Information: (910) 205-1299

**Phoenix International Raceway**
P.O. Box 13088
Phoenix, AZ 85002
Tickets: (602) 252-2227
Information: (602) 252-3833

**Pocono Raceway**
P.O. Box 500
Long Pond, PA 18334
Tickets: 800-722-3929
Information: (717) 646-2300

**Richmond International Raceway**
P.O. Box 9257
Richmond, VA 23222
Tickets & Information: (804) 345-7223

**Sears Point Raceway**
Hwys. 37 and 121
Sonoma, CA 95476
Tickets: 800-870-7223
Information: (707) 938-8448

**Talladega Superspeedway**
P.O. Box 777
Talladega, AL 35160
Tickets: (205) 362-9064
Information: (205) 362-2261

**Texas Motor Speedway**
P.O. Box 500
Fort Worth, TX 76101-2500
Tickets: (817) 215-8500
Information: (817) 215-8520

**Watkins Glen International**
P.O. Box 500
Watkins Glen, NY 14891
Tickets: (607) 535-2481
Information: (607) 535-2486

## Television/Radio Networks

**ABC Sports**
47 West 66th St.
New York, NY 10023
(212) 456-4867

**CBS Sports**
51 West 52nd St.
30th Floor
New York, NY 10019
(212) 975-4321

**ESPN/ESPN2**
ESPN Plaza
935 Middle St.
Bristol, CT 06010
(203) 585-2000

**Motor Racing Network (MRN)**
1801 International Speedway Blvd.
Daytona Beach, FL 32114
(904) 254-6760

**Performance Racing Network (PRN)**
P.O. Box 600
Concord, NC 28026-0600
(704) 455-3228

**The Nashville Network (TNN)**
2806 Opryland Dr.
Nashville, TN 37214
(615) 889-6840

**FOX Sportsnet Speedvision**
2 Stamford Plaza, 9th Floor
281 Tresser Blvd.
Stamford, CT 06901

**TBS Superstation**
One CNN Center
Atlanta, GA 30348
(404) 827-1717

*Television and radio reporters rush to get the scoop.*

## NASCAR Licensed Television and Radio Shows

**Inside NASCAR**
TNN

**Inside Winston Cup Racing**
Speedvision

**NASCAR Country**
Nationally syndicated radio show

**NASCAR Garage (television)**
TNN

**NASCAR Garage (radio)**
MRN

**NASCAR Live**
Radio show on more than 250 stations

**NASCAR Raceweek**
Speedvision

**NASCAR ShopTalk**
ESPN and ESPN2

**NASCAR 2day**
ESPN and ESPN2

**NASCAR Today**
Radio newscast on more than 300 stations

**This Week in NASCAR**
FOX Sports

## Publications

**Inside NASCAR**
888 W. Big Beaver
Suite 600
Troy, MI 48084
(810) 362-7400

**NASCAR Preview and Press Guide**
P.O. Box 30036
Charlotte, NC 28230-0036

**NASCAR Racing for Teens**
P.O. Box 588
Concord, NC 28025
(704) 786-7132

**NASCAR Trucks**
Petersen Publishing
6420 Wilshire Blvd.
Los Angeles, CA 90048
Subscriptions: (213) 782-2000

**NASCAR Winston Cup Illustrated**
128 South Tryon St.
Suite 2275
Charlotte, NC 28202
(704) 371-3966

**NASCAR Winston Cup Scene**
128 South Tryon St.
Suite 2275
Charlotte, NC 28202
(704) 371-3966

**Professional NASCAR Garage Magazine**
Babcox Publications
11 South Forge St.
Akron, OH 44304

## Miscellaneous

**Motor Racing Outreach**
Smith Tower
Suite 336
Harrisburg, NC 28075
(704) 455-3828

**NASCAR**
P.O. Box 2875
Daytona Beach, FL 32120
(904) 253-0611

**NASCAR Online**
www.nascar.com

**Winston Cup Racing Wives Auxiliary**
P.O. Box 251
Harrisburg, NC 28075

## Fan Clubs

**Bobby Allison**
6616 Walmsley Blvd.
Richmond, VA 23224

**John Andretti**
2416 Music Valley Dr.
Suite 161
Nashville, TN 37214

**Johnny Benson**
3102 Bird NE
Grand Rapids, MI 49505

**Brett Bodine**
304 Performance Rd.
Mooresville, NC 28115

**Geoff Bodine**
P.O. Box 1790
Monroe, NC 28111-1790

**Todd Bodine**
P.O. Box 2427
Cornelius, NC 28031

**Jeff Burton**
P.O. Box 1160
Halifax, VA 24558

**Ward Burton**
c/o The Source International
3475 Myer Lee Dr. NE
Winston-Salem, NC 27101

**Ricky Craven**
P.O. Box 472
Concord, NC 28026

**Dale Earnhardt**
5301 West W. T. Harris Blvd.
Charlotte, NC 28269

**Bill Elliott**
P.O. Box 248
Dawsonville, GA 30534

**Jeff Gordon**
514 E Route 66
P.O. Box 515
Williams, AZ 86046-0515

**Steve Grissom**
P.O. Box 989
Statesville, NC 28687

**Bobby Hamilton**
c/o Petty Enterprises
311 Branson Mill Rd.
Randleman, NC 27317

**Ernie Irvan**
1027 Central Dr.
Concord, NC 28027

**Dale Jarrett**
P.O. Box 564
Conover, NC 28613

**Bobby Labonte**
P.O. Box 358
Trinity, NC 27370

**Terry Labonte**
P.O. Box 843
Trinity, NC 27370

**Chad Little**
P.O. Box 562323
Charlotte, NC 28256

**Sterling Marlin**
1116 W. 7th St.
Suite 62
Columbia, TN 38401

**Mark Martin**
P.O. Box 68
Ash Flat, AR 72513

**Rick Mast**
Route 6 Box 224A
Lexington, VA 24450

**Jeremy Mayfield**
P.O. Box 2365
Cornelius, NC 28031

**Ted Musgrave**
P.O. Box 1089
Liberty, NC 27298

**Joe Nemechek**
c/o Nemco Motorsports
P.O. Box 1131
Mooresville, NC 28115

**Kyle Petty**
135 Longfield Dr.
Mooresville, NC 28115

**Richard Petty**
1028 E 22nd St.
Kannapolis, NC 28083

**Ricky Rudd**
P.O. Box 7586
Richmond, VA 23231

**Ken Schrader**
P.O. Box 1227
Kannapolis, NC 28082

**Morgan Shepherd**
P.O. Box 1456
Stow, OH 44224-1456

**Lake Speed**
P.O. Box 499
Danville, WV 25053

**Jimmy Spencer**
P.O. Box 1626
Mooresville, NC 28115

**Hut Stricklin**
P.O. Box 1028
Calera, AL 35040

**Dick Trickle**
5415 Vesuvius Furnace Rd.
Iron Station, NC 28080

**Kenny Wallace**
P.O. Box 3050
Concord, NC 28025

**Rusty Wallace**
224 Rolling Hills Rd.
Suite 5A
Mooresville, NC 28115

**Darrell Waltrip**
P.O. Box 381
Harrisburg, NC 28075

**Michael Waltrip**
P.O. Box 339
Sherrills Ford, NC 28673

# A RACING GLOSSARY

Every trade, profession, and art has its own jargon or special "language" filled with words and phrases particular to it. Racing is no different, and the colorful and dynamic nature of the sport is reflected in the terms used by the competitors. However, it's easy for an "outsider" to become confused when faced with a barrage of this so-called tech talk.

Here's a glossary of terms and words unique to NASCAR Winston Cup racing.

***Aerodynamics***—As applied to racing, the study of airflow and the forces of resistance and pressure that result from the flow of air over, under, and around a moving car.

***A-frame***—Either upper or lower connecting suspension piece (in the shape of an A) locking the frame to the spindle.

***Air box***—Housing for the air cleaner that connects the air intake at the base of the windshield to the carburetor.

***Air filter***—Paper or gauze element used to prevent dirt from entering the engine. Located in the air box.

***Air dam***—Extension below the front bumper of the race car that affects aerodynamics.

***Alternator***—A belt-driven device mounted on the front of the engine that recharges the battery while the engine is running.

***A-post***—The post extending from the roof line to the base of the windshield on either side of the car.

***Apron***—The paved portion of a race track that separates the racing surface from the (usually unpaved) infield.

***Axle***—Rotating shafts connecting the rear differential gears to the rear wheels.

***Ball joint***—A ball inside a socket that can turn and pivot in any direction. Used to allow the suspension to travel while the driver steers the car.

***Banjo chassis***—Named for its designer, Banjo Matthews. Widely used in NASCAR Winston Cup racing in the 1960s, '70s, and '80s.

***Banking***—The sloping of a race track, particularly at a curve or corner, from the apron to the outside wall. Degree of banking refers to the height of a track's slope at its outside edge.

***Bear grease***—Slang term used to describe any patching material used to fill cracks and holes or smooth bumps on a track's surface. Can also be used as a sealer on the track.

***Bellhousing***—A cover, shaped like a bell, that surrounds the flywheel/clutch that connects the engine to the transmission.

***Bias-ply***—Layers of fabric within a tire that are woven in angles. Also used as a term to describe tires made in this manner. Last used in NASCAR Winston Cup racing in 1992.

***Binders***—Brakes.

***Bite***—(1) "Round of bite" describes the turning or adjusting of a car's jacking screws found at each wheel. "Weight jacking" distributes the car's weight at each wheel. (2) Adhesion of a tire to the track surface. See "Slick."

***Bleeder valve***—A valve in the wheel used to reduce air pressure in tires. Bleeder valves are not approved for NASCAR Winston Cup racing.

***Blend line***—Line painted on the track near the apron and extending from the pit road exit into the first turn. When leaving the pits a driver must stay below it to safely "blend" back into traffic.

***Blown motor***—Major-league engine failure, for instance, when a connecting rod goes through the engine block producing a lot of smoke and steam.

***Bore***—Pistons travel up and down within each cylinder, or bore, in the engine block.

**B-post**—Post extending from the roof line to the base of window behind the driver's head.

**Brake caliper**—The part of the brake system that, when applied by the driver, clamps the brake disc/rotor to slow or stop the car. There is one on each wheel of a NASCAR Winston Cup car.

**Camber**—The amount a tire is tilted in or out from vertical. Described in degrees, either positive or negative.

**Camshaft**—A rotating shaft within the engine that opens and closes the intake and exhaust valves in the engine.

**Carburetor**—A device connected directly to the gas pedal and mounted on top of the engine.

**Chassis**—The steel structure or frame of the car.

**Chute**—A race track straight-away.

**Compound**—A formula or "recipe" of rubber composing a particular tire. Different tracks require different tire compounds. "Left-side" tires are considerably softer than "right-side" tires and it's against the rules to run left sides on the right.

**Compression ratio**—Amount that the air/fuel mixture is compressed as the piston reaches the top of the bore. The higher the compression, the more the horsepower.

**Cowl**—A removable metal scoop at the base of the windshield and rear of the hood that directs air into the air box.

**C-post**—The post extending from the roof line to the base of the rear window to the top of the deck lid.

**Crankcase**—The area of the engine block that houses the crankshaft.

**Crankshaft**—The rotating shaft within the engine that delivers the power from the pistons to the flywheel.

**Cubic-inch displacement**—The size of an engine measured in cubic inches. The maximum size for a NASCAR Winston Cup engine is 358.000 cubic inches.

**Cylinder head**—Made of aluminum, it is bolted to the top of each side of the engine block. Cylinder heads hold the valves and spark plugs. Passages through the heads make up the intake and exhaust ports.

**Deck lid**—The trunk lid.

**Dirty air**—Turbulent air caused by fast-moving cars that can cause a particular car to lose control.

*The "war wagon" stores a team's essential equipment in the pits.*

**Downforce**—The downward force the car receives when moving through the air. Helps a car "hug" or "stick" to a race track.

**Draft**—When one car follows another closely, allowing the one in front to cut through the air providing a cleaner path through the air, i.e., less resistance, for the car in back.

**Drafting**—The practice of two or more cars, while racing, to run nose to tail, almost touching. The lead car, by displacing air in front of it, creates a vacuum between its rear end and the following car's nose. The second car is actually pulled by the first.

**Drag**—The resistance a car experiences when passing through air. A resisting force exerted on a car parallel to its airstream and opposite in direction to its motion.

**Driveshaft**—The steel tube that connects the transmission to the rear end housing.

**Dyno**—Shortened form of "dynamometer," a machine used to measure an engine's horsepower.

**Engine Block**—An iron casting from the manufacturer that envelops the crankshaft, connecting rods and pistons. Aluminum engine blocks are not allowed in NASCAR Winston Cup racing.

**Equalize**—Cars in superspeedway races are required to run tires with both inner tubes and "inner liners," which are actually small tires inside the standard tires. When the inner liner loses air pressure and that pressure becomes the same as that within the outer tire, the tire is said to have equalized and a vibration is created.

**Esses**—On a road course, a series of acute left- and right-hand turns, one turn immediately following another.

***"Factory"***—A term designating the "Big Three" auto manufacturers: General Motors, Ford, and Chrysler. The "factory days" refer to periods in the 1950s and '60s when the manufacturers actively and openly provided sponsorship money and technical support to some race teams.

***Fan***—A fan is used to pull air through a radiator or oil cooler. Heat is transferred from the hot oil or water in the radiator to the moving air.

***Flat-out***—Racing a car as fast as possible under given conditions.

***Flywheel***—A heavy metal rotating wheel that is part of the clutch system used to keep elements such as the crankshaft turning steadily.

***Four-barrel***—The type of carburetor used in NASCAR Winston Cup racing.

***Frame***—The metal "skeleton" or structure of a car on which the sheet metal is formed. Also referred to as a chassis.

***Front-steer***—A car in which the steering components (box, etc.) are located ahead of the front axle.

***Fuel***—Gasoline. NASCAR Winston Cup competitors use only 76 racing gasoline.

***Fuel cell***—A holding tank for gasoline. Consists of a metal "box" that contains a flexible tear-resistant bladder and foam baffling. A product of aerospace technology, it's designed to eliminate or minimize fuel spillage.

***Fuel pump***—Pumps fuel from the fuel cell through the fuel line into the carburetor.

***Gasket***—A thin material, made of paper, silicone, or metal, used as a seal between two similar machined metal surfaces such as cylinder heads and the engine block.

*New tires, or "stickers," still have the manufacturer's adhesive label.*

***Gauge***—An instrument, usually mounted on the dashboard, used to monitor engine conditions such as fuel pressure and temperature, oil pressure and temperature, and RPM (revolutions per minute).

***Gears***—Circular, wheel-shaped parts with teeth along the edges. The interlocking of two of these mechanisms enables one to turn the other.

***Greenhouse***—The upper area of a car that extends from the base of the windshield in the front, the tops of the doors on the sides, and the base of the rear window in the back. Includes all of a, b, and c pillars, the entire glass area, and the car's roof or top.

***Groove***—The best route around a race track; the most efficient or quickest way around the track for a particular driver. The "high groove" takes a car closer to the outside wall for most of a lap. The "low groove" takes a car closer to the apron than the outside wall. Road racers use the term "line." Drivers search for a fast groove.

***Harmonic balancer***—An element used to reduce vibration in the crankshaft.

**Handling**—Generally, a car's performance while racing, qualifying, or practicing. How a car "handles" is determined by its tires, suspension geometry, aerodynamics, and other factors.

**Horsepower**—A measurement of mechanical or engine power. Measured in the amount of power it takes to move 33,000 pounds one foot in a minute.

**Ignition**—An electrical system used to ignite the fuel mix in an internal combustion engine.

**"Independent"**—A driver or team owner who does not have financial backing from a major sponsor and must make do with second-hand equipment such as parts and tires. The term, like the breed, is becoming rarer every year.

**Intake manifold**—A housing that directs the fuel/air mixture through the port openings in the cylinder heads.

**Jet**—When air is sent at a high velocity through the carburetor, jets direct the fuel into the airstream. Jets are made slightly larger to make a richer mixture or slightly smaller to make a more lean mixture, depending on track and weather conditions.

**Line**—See "Groove."

**Loose**—When the rear tires of the car have trouble sticking in the corners.

**"Loose stuff"**—Debris such as sand, pebbles, or small pieces of rubber that tend to collect on a track's apron or near the outside wall.

**Lug nuts**—Large nuts applied with a high-pressure air wrench to wheels during a pit stop to secure the tires in place.

**Magnaflux**—Short for "magnetic particle inspection." A procedure for checking all ferrous (steel) parts—suspension pieces, connecting rods, cylinder heads, etc.—for cracks and other defects utilizing a solution of metal particles and fluorescent dye and a black light. Surface cracks will appear as red lines.

**Marbles**—Excess rubber buildup above the upper groove on the race track.

**Neutral**—A term drivers use when referring to how their car is handling. When a car is neither loose nor pushing.

**Oil pump**—It pumps oil to lubricate all moving engine parts.

**"P&G"**—Basically, the procedure for checking the cubic-inch displacement of an engine. The term comes from the manufacturer of the particular gauge used.

**Panhard bar**—A lateral bar that keeps the rear tires centered within body of car (connects to the frame on one side and the rear axle on the other). Also called a track bar.

**Piston**—A circular element that moves up and down in the cylinder compressing the air/fuel mixture in the top of the chamber, helping to produce horsepower.

**Post-entry (PE)**—A team or driver who submits an entry blank for a race after the deadline for submission has passed. A post-entry receives no NASCAR Winston Cup points.

**Push**—See "Tight."

**Quarter panel**—The sheet metal on both sides of the car from the C-post to the rear bumper below the deck lid and above the wheel well.

**Rear-steer**—A car in which the steering components are located behind the front axle.

**Restrictor plate**—A thin metal plate with four holes that restrict airflow from the carburetor into the engine. Used to reduce horsepower. The restrictor plates are currently used at Daytona International Speedway and Talladega Superspeedway.

**RPM**—Revolutions per minute of the engine's crankshaft.

**Scuffs**—Tires that have been used at least once and are saved for further racing. A lap or two is enough to "scuff" them in. Most often used in qualifying.

**Short track**—A speedway under one mile in distance.

**Slick**—A track condition where, for a number of reasons, it's hard for a car's tires to adhere to the surface or get a good "bite." A slick race track is not necessarily wet or slippery because of oil, water, etc.

**Slingshot**—A maneuver in which a car following the leader in a draft suddenly steers around it, breaking the vacuum; this provides an extra burst of speed that allows the second car to take the lead. See "Drafting."

**Spoiler**—A metal blade attached to the rear deck lid of a car. It helps restrict air flow over the rear of the car.

**Sponsor**—An individual or business establishment that financially supports a race driver, team, race, or series of races in return for advertising and marketing benefits.

**Stagger**—The difference in size between the tires on the left and right sides of a car. Because of a tire's makeup, slight variations in circumference result. Stagger between right-side and left-side tires may range from less than a half inch to more than an inch. Stagger applies to only bias-ply tires and not to radials.

**Stick**—Tire traction. "The car's sticking to the track."

**Stickers**—New tires that still have the factory sticker on them.

**Stroking**—Said of a driver who allegedly "lays back" in a race so as not to punish or wear out equipment before the end of an event.

**Superspeedway**—A race track of a mile or more in distance. Road courses are included. NOTE: Racers refer to three types of oval tracks. Short tracks are under a mile, "intermediate" tracks are at least a mile but under two miles, and "speedways" are two miles and longer.

**Sway Bar**—Or antiroll bar. Bar used to resist or counteract the rolling force of the car body through the turns.

**Tight**—When the front of the car has difficulty turning into the corners.

**Track bar**—See "Panhard bar."

**Trailing arm**—A rear suspension piece holding the rear axle firmly fore and aft yet allowing it to travel up and down.

**Tri-oval**—A race track that has a "hump" or "fifth turn" in addition to the standard four corners. Not to be confused with a triangle-shaped speedway, which has only three distinct corners.

**200 mph tape**—"Racer's tape." Duct tape so strong, it will hold a banged-up race car together long enough to finish a race.

**Wedge, round of**—Adjusting the handling of the car by altering pressure on the rear springs.

**Wrench**—Slang for racing mechanic.

# Sarah Saw A Blue Macaw

Jo Ellen Bogart
Sylvie Daigneault

Scholastic Canada
Toronto • Sydney • New York • London • Auckland

**Scholastic Canada Ltd.**
123 Newkirk Road, Richmond Hill, Ontario, Canada L4C 3G5
**Scholastic Inc.**
555 Broadway, New York, NY 10012, USA
**Scholastic Australia Pty Limited**
PO Box 579, Gosford, NSW 2250, Australia
**Scholastic New Zealand Limited**
Private Bag 94407, Greenmount, Auckland, New Zealand
**Scholastic Ltd.**
Villiers House, Clarendon Avenue, Leamington Spa,
Warwickshire CV32 5PR, UK



8 7 6 5 4 Printed and bound in Canada 6 7 8 9 /9

**Canadian Cataloguing in Publication Data**

Bogart, Jo Ellen, 1945-
Sarah saw a blue macaw

ISBN 0-590-73227-7

I. Daigneault, Sylvie. II. Title.

PS8553.0465S37 1991 jC813'.54 C90-095459-0
PZ7.B64Sa 1991

To Jean Little, for her love of words.
J.E.B.
For the rainforest — may it always be beautiful.
S.D.

Where did Sarah swing?
Sarah swung where branches hung.
Big branches hung where Sarah swung
And trees were towering.

What did Sarah see?
Sarah saw a blue macaw.
The blue macaw that Sarah saw
Was sleeping in a tree.

When did Maggie wake?
Maggie woke when branches broke.
The branches broke and Maggie woke
When Terence made them shake.

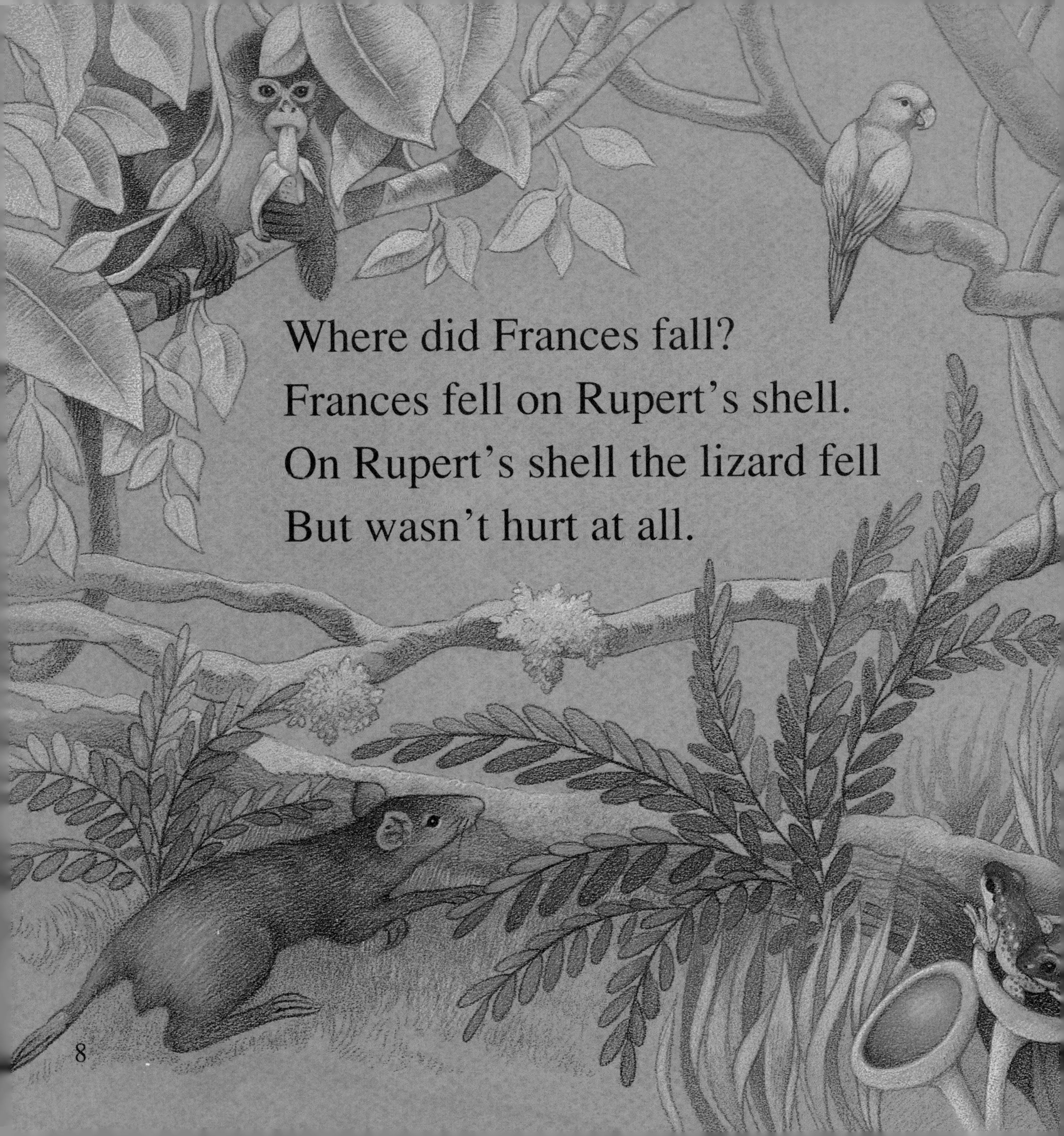

Where did Frances fall?
Frances fell on Rupert's shell.
On Rupert's shell the lizard fell
But wasn't hurt at all.

Where did Daniel drink?
Daniel drank down on the bank.
And on the bank where Daniel drank,
He saw a tiny skink.

How did Sherman swim?
Sherman swam as fast as Sam.
As fast as Sam he surely swam,
But not as fast as Kim.

What did Hannah hear?
Hannah heard a hummingbird.
The hummingbird that Hannah heard
Was very, very near.

Where did Katie sleep?
Katie slept where spiders crept.
The spiders crept where Katie slept,
But never made a peep.

What did Jacob take?
Jacob took another look.
Another look was what he took,
And saw a hidden snake.

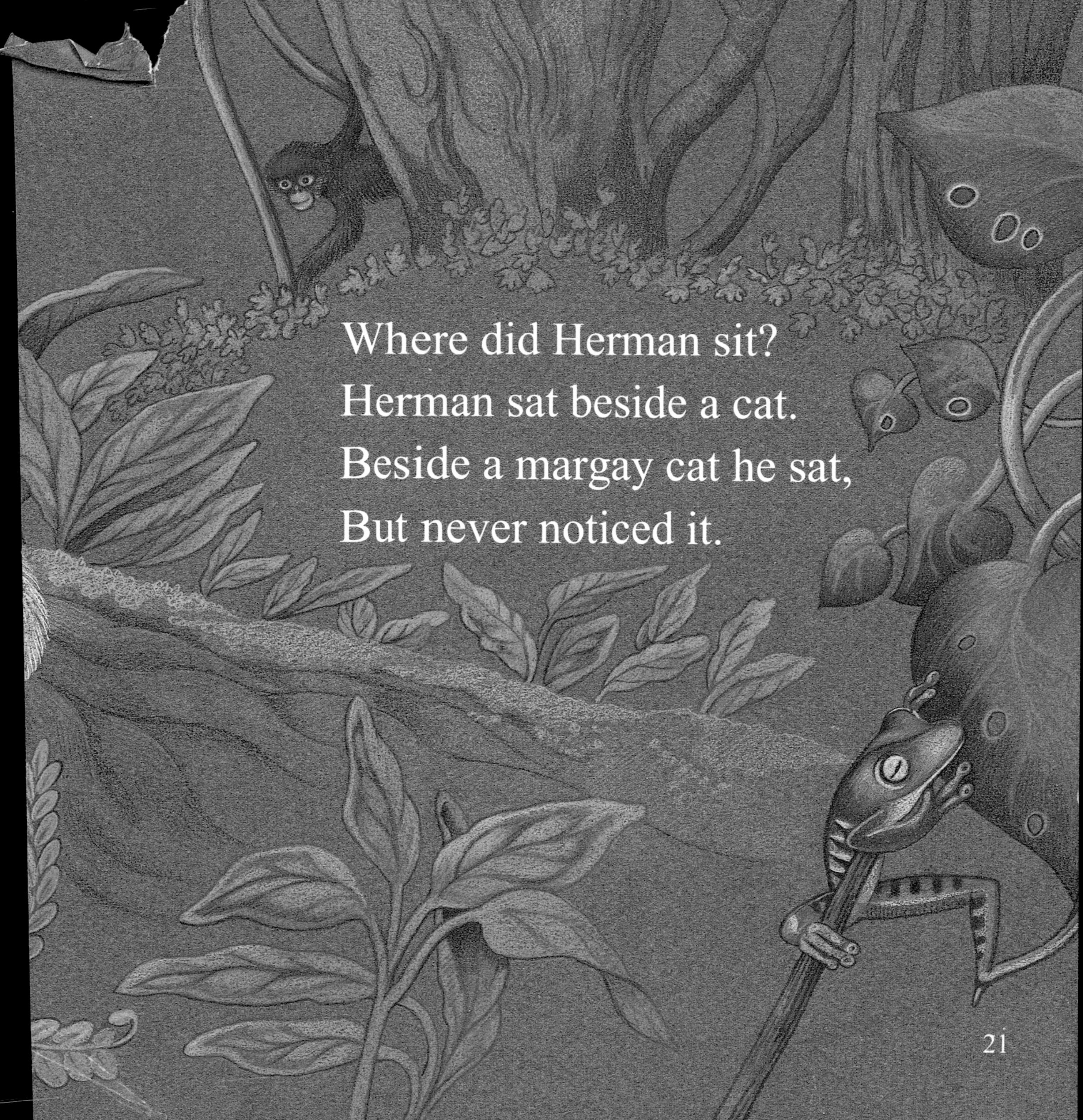

Where did Herman sit?
Herman sat beside a cat.
Beside a margay cat he sat,
But never noticed it.

What did Charlie choose?
Charlie chose a clever pose.
The clever pose that Charlie chose
Was trickier than Sue's.

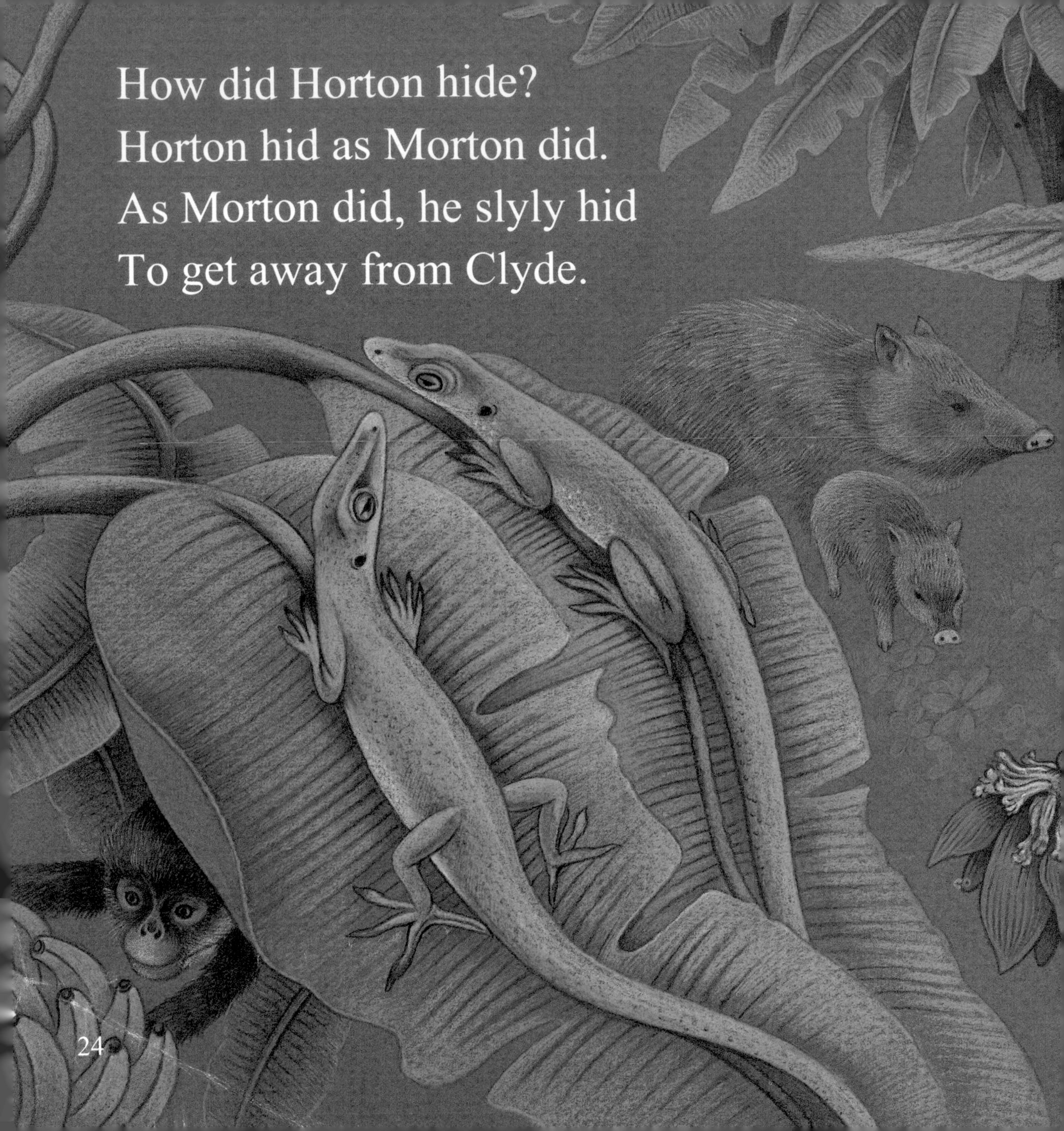

How did Horton hide?
Horton hid as Morton did.
As Morton did, he slyly hid
To get away from Clyde.

What did Mona ride?
Mona rode a giant toad.
The giant toad that Mona rode
Had such a bumpy hide.

How did Franklin fly?
Franklin flew on wings of blue.
On wings of blue he lightly flew
To places in the sky.

What did Sarah say?
Sarah said, "It's time for bed."
"I'm off to bed now," Sarah said.
"Tomorrow we will play."

# Cast of Characters

You can spot Sarah in every picture.

***Pages 4-5:*** Sarah is a spider monkey. You can also find a silky anteater, blue and yellow macaws, a squirrel monkey and a butterfly.

***Pages 6-7:*** Maggie is a blue and yellow macaw. Terence is a tree porcupine. You can also find tanagers, a bat and a three-toed sloth with her baby.

***Pages 8-9:*** Frances is an iguana. Rupert is a yellow-legged tortoise.You can also find two cobalt-winged parakeets, an agouti and two arrow-poison frogs.

***Pages 10-11:*** Daniel is a Brazilian tapir.You can also find a baby tapir, a nest of barred antshrikes, a skink and a frog.

***Pages 12-13:*** Sherman, Sam and Kim are giant otters.You can also find a paca and a jaguar.

***Pages 14-15:*** Hannah is a capybara. You can also find a hummingbird, a frog and a blue-crowned motmot.

***Pages 16-17:*** Katie is a kinkajou.You can also find a red howler monkey, an umbrella bird, two spiders and a butterfly.

***Pages 18-19:*** Jacob is a toco toucan.You can also find an emerald tree boa, a pale-headed saki, a cobalt-winged parakeet and a marsupial frog.

***Pages 20-21:*** Herman is a white-fronted capuchin monkey.You can also find a margay, a three-toed sloth and a tree frog.

***Pages 22-23:*** Charlie and Sue are great potoos. You can also find red howler monkeys and a blue and yellow macaw.

***Pages 24-25:*** Horton and Morton are anoles. Clyde is a coati.You can also find two collared peccaries.

***Pages 26-27:*** Mona is a pygmy marmoset. You can also find a giant toad and two tinamous.

***Pages 28-29:*** Franklin is a morpho butterfly. You can also find a silky anteater with her baby.

***Pages 30-31:*** Sarah joins two other spider monkeys. You can also find a margay, a yellow tree frog and a giant armadillo.